No Need for Sight When You Have a VISION

No Need for Sight When You Have a VISION

What Blindness Can Teach Us about Risk and Leadership

LEX GILLETTE

No Need for Sight When You Have a Vision
What Blindness Can Teach Us about Risk and Leadership

ISBN 978-1-5445-3188-5 Hardcover
978-1-5445-3187-8 Paperback
978-1-5445-3186-1 Ebook

To my mom.

Long before anyone else gave me a shot,
you were the one who saw potential in me, didn't let me
give up on myself, and didn't let me use excuses.
You expected of me everything you would have expected
of a child who had sight, and that set the framework
for being able to acquire my own vision.

CONTENTS

INTRODUCTION ix

1. MAP WHAT YOU KNOW TO EXPLORE THE UNKNOWN 1

2. BECOME NUMB TO "NO" 15

3. STOP WORRYING ABOUT BLENDING IN –OR STANDING OUT 35

4. ARE YOU A CATALYST? 55

5. SET YOUR VISION 67

6. VULNERABILITY IS THE KEY TO EFFECTIVE TEAMWORK 87

7. WHO FUELS YOUR VISION? 99

8. YOUR VOICE IS A GUIDE 125

9. MOVE MOUNTAINS BY LEARNING TO FEEL . . . 149

10. YOUR COURAGE IS JUST BEYOND YOUR FEAR. 161

11. WHEN VISION NEEDS A REVISION 183

12. FOCUS ON THE WIN 207

CONCLUSION. 237

ABOUT THE AUTHOR. 249

INTRODUCTION

If you were to suddenly lose your sight, what would you miss seeing the most?

I remember riding my bike as a kid, and seeing the street stretch ahead of me for what seemed like forever. I remember seeing the world spin as I went into a cartwheel in the green grass in front of my house. I played video games, my eyes glued to the TV screen as I watched the brightly colored football jerseys streak toward the goal line. I remember seeing my mom smile at me during dinner, a picture of *The Last Supper* hanging on the wall behind her.

And I remember the day when, at seven years old, I got out of the bath, looked in the bathroom mirror, and could barely see my own face.

I rubbed my eyes and blinked, but my sight was still blurry. There were dark spots where my eyes and eyebrows were. I could see the color of my complexion and the shadow of my cheekbones, but nothing was clear. I looked from my face to my hands, and then up at the lights on the ceiling, but there were no sharp lines. Everything was fuzzy, like my eyes couldn't focus properly.

I went to my mom and told her something was terribly wrong.

She thought I had gotten something in my eyes when I was playing outside, so she flushed my eyes out with eye drops. The drops didn't help. She told me to get some sleep. We hoped everything would return to normal in the morning.

But when I woke up, nothing had changed. My mom took me to the doctor, who told us that I needed an emergency operation to fix my detached retina.

I was optimistic going into that first operation. The doctors told me that everything was going to be fine, that they would go in and fix the issue. It seemed like they had a firm handle on the situation, so I put my trust in their hands.

After the first operation, I could see well for about three or four weeks, but then my sight began to get blurry again—even a little worse than before. The second examination revealed that I would need another operation to repair a retina detachment.

The second operation seemed like a success. Again, I could see well for another three to four weeks. But after that, my sight got even blurrier.

That was the pattern for my eighth year of life: operations, brief periods of sight, then the return of the blurriness that got progressively worse. After the thirteenth—and final—operation, the doctors told me that they had exhausted all the options. There was nothing else they could do to help my sight.

I went home, went through my daily routine, went to sleep each night...and every morning, I was able to see less than I could the day before. Gradually I lost my sight.

And then the day arrived when I woke up and was unable to see anything.

What I learned from that point forward—what I want to teach you in this book—was that I never had to be defined by my limitations. Without sight, I learned to use my vision to bring my dreams into reality.

At age eight, I never would have dreamed I would become a record-holding athlete and a five-time Paralympic medalist. But as I was about to learn, our limitations are just perceptions. Everyone has the ability to bring dreams to reality, to create a life much bigger than they can imagine.

This has been the most powerful lesson of my life, but it would take me awhile to learn.

My New Normal

The reality of my blindness hit me in the chest.

I could no longer see my neighborhood, but I remembered where the streetlights were, where the tree house was, where all the stairs were up to the houses—even though I couldn't see them anymore. I could no longer see to read, write, or draw pictures. I couldn't see well enough to play video games. And I couldn't see my mom anymore, the person who took me to the pool, read with me, and played catch with me at the park.

If you were to suddenly lose your sight, who would you miss seeing the most?

My mom was my role model—not just because she is a great parent, but because she is a great example of what it means to be a go-getter and to refuse to be defined by limitations. Like me, my mom is visually impaired, in her case from glaucoma. She taught me to not allow the rest of the world to dictate what I was going to do or who I was going to become.

"I want to make sure you can go into the world and achieve the things you want," she told me. "We all need help at some point, but there are a lot of things you're going to need to do for yourself. Don't allow others to take on those responsibilities—those are *your* responsibilities. You handle your business."

After I went through the grieving process of losing my sight, I had a lot to learn: how to get to my classrooms by myself, how to get to the gym, to the cafeteria, to the school bus, to the front door, to the house. I eventually learned how to read Braille and use a cane. I still had to do chores, so I had to learn how to clean my room, take out the trash, and wash dishes.

Most importantly, I learned that even though I'd lost one of my five senses, I still had other abilities and skills I could tap into that would help me compensate for what I'd lost, help me rise up and overcome. That knowledge set the framework for my success.

Everything changed drastically when I got to high school and was introduced to my teacher of the visually impaired, Brian Whitmer. He assisted me during PE class, making sure that I had everything I needed to participate alongside my sighted peers. He introduced me to Paralympic sport, and painted the picture of the kind of athletic career I could have someday, representing Team USA in competitions across the world.

His guidance lit a fire under me to turn that dream into reality. I learned to compete in the long jump and sprint events, using guides to orient me on the track and give me auditory cues. The rest is history.

Over more than a decade of athletic competition, I've won gold medals in the World Para Athletics Championships and the Parapan American Games, and five silver medals at the Paralympic Games. I've yet to win the elusive gold at the Paralympics, but my fire is still lit. I'm going to work hard to get the gold in the Paris 2024 Paralympic Games. That's perseverance in its purest form: when you know your goal will challenge what you think is possible. Perseverance is continuing to push forward through adversity because you believe in the vision on the other side of your obstacle.

Put On Your Blindfolds

If you were to suddenly lose your sight, how would you learn to tap into your vision?

A few years ago, I stood in front of a group of emerging leaders—people like you who wanted to break through their own limitations to make their dreams a reality—and I told them my story. Then I said, "It's your turn to experience a day in my life. I'm going to teach you how to run blind."

The blindfold I wear when I compete is a requirement of the competition, to ensure that there is a level playing field among athletes whose sight is impaired in different ways. Everyone wears a blindfold to ensure that sight isn't a competitive advantage—although, in many ways, sight isn't that much of an advantage. It is your *vision*—your ability to see beyond that blindfold, to see beyond what is in existence, to close the gap between where you currently are and where your vision lies—that affords you the real advantage.

When I compete, I explained, I never do it alone. I have my guide, Wesley Williams, with me. As you work toward your own vision of the future, you need collaborators in your corner. By facilitating a guide running experience for the participants, I knew I could help them see how to connect with others to reach their goals.

I told them, "One person is going to be the athlete and the other person is going to be the guide: we're going to tap into the teamwork aspect and break down what it really takes to become a dynamic duo."

But before they put on their blindfolds, I asked, "What does it take to be a highly successful team?"

From a high-level standpoint, effective collaboration takes trust, communication, vulnerability, and empathy. You need to trust others, but you also need to trust yourself and your abilities. When you communicate, you need to know what to say, the right time to say it, and the best way to say it so it can be received. You have to be willing to be vulnerable and put yourself out there, so your collaborator knows what you're dealing with. Empathy is needed to understand the other person's experience as you work together.

Anytime two people work together in a new situation, the first few sessions are a great time to learn and understand each other. "It's not always a comfortable experience to establish that foundation," I told the group. "You may have to speak up more than you're used to, and tell your guide directly what you need. Each of you might feel timid, worried about seeming rude or insensitive. But these conversations are important to learn how to treat each other and how to get on the same page to accomplish your goals together."

"When someone does that for me, I feel amazing around that person," I added. "That's a motivator, a confidence booster for both of us, so we're able to show up in that space, ready to rock and roll. All those traits you're working on today—trust, communication, vulnerability, and empathy—play a huge part in being a great leader as well."

As the participants were about to learn, this workshop wasn't just about running together. It was about *winning* together as an incredible team.

On Your Marks

Once the participants put the blindfolds on, people automatically put their hands out in front of them, reaching into the space they couldn't see anymore. They were disoriented and paralyzed, stuck in one spot. Like most people, they were so used to getting visual data through their eyesight that they needed to learn how to focus on their other senses and abilities. With the blindfold on, they'd entered a space of total vulnerability, and they described feeling very exposed.

We navigated to the starting line, with the blindfolded participants serving as the athletes and those who were not blindfolded serving as their guides. I told them, "We're going to work on running from the starting line to the finish, about thirty meters away. If you're not wearing a blindfold, you're going to be tasked with guiding your athlete from the starting line to the finish line."

I reminded them that their athlete would use the guide's words to navigate. If you are running blindfolded, you don't want to hear your guide say, "Oh, shoot!" You might think there's something in your lane or something you could trip over. If you're the guide, you don't want to say something that could cause the athlete to come to an abrupt stop, resulting in them not completing the run. You also want to give the athlete careful direction so they have a good idea of where they are in the race.

We used the first round for practice. We gave each blindfolded person a chance to get acclimated to walking, jogging, and running without sight. They held onto a tether—a piece of fabric connecting them to their guide—so they could feel feedback from their guide's movements as they ran alongside them.

Afterward, we debriefed: "What did it feel like? What did you realize in that experience? What could you have done differently to guide your athlete? Or, if you were the athlete, what could your guide have done differently to help you feel more comfortable?"

A lot of the blindfolded athletes said, "Oh my gosh, that was crazy," or "That was so scary!"

Many of the guides acknowledged, "I did a terrible job at guiding you! I didn't keep you inside the lane. This is so hard. I was so afraid of saying the wrong thing, or of doing something that would get you hurt."

The athletes thought they might trip over something or get their legs tangled up, and they said it was hard to move as freely as they normally did without the blindfold.

Then we had the duos trade places, so the guide became the athlete and the athlete became the guide, and they tried the exercise again.

Next, instead of having the guide tethered to the athlete, we set it up like a long jump. We didn't do an actual jump, but we had the guide at the end of the runway, with the athlete at the starting mark, and the guide had to clap and yell so the athlete knew where to run.

Without being connected to the other person, the athlete had to listen to their guide's voice and run toward it. The pressure was on for the guides, who had to give their athletes clear directions from a distance. For someone who can't see, it's pointless to say, "Go over there." You have to be more explicit and specific: "You need to move to your right-hand side, take one step to your right, or take two steps back." They had to think about the experience from the athlete's perspective, or they would risk giving the wrong directions and running their athlete off course.

Through the running and jumping exercises, both the athletes and the guides slowly learned to shift their focus away from the limitations of the situation and toward all the resources they could use to communicate and come up with solutions to achieve their goals.

This opportunity gave them a temporary glimpse into considering: "What else can I draw on? How else can I be creative? What are the other options that are available to me?"

After our practice sessions, we had the participants compete. We explained the rules: They would run in pairs again, athlete tethered to guide. Just like in Paralympic competition, they had to stay connected, they had to stay in their designated lanes, and the athlete had to cross the finish line first, before their guide.

With the announcement of the competition, their mindsets shifted. Whereas moments before, they had felt unsure and overwhelmed, they suddenly became amped up and excited to be the first to cross the finish line.

We lined them up at the starting line. "On your mark!" one of the facilitators shouted. "Set!" Everyone went silent.

"Go!"

Most groups started bolting. All of them shouted to each other: "Come on, come on, let's go!"

By the time they crossed the finish line, they were laughing the kind of fun, childlike laughter that spills forth when you're a kid running around outside with your friends. They were learning difficult lessons about trust and communication, but having fun at the same time.

As we get older, we tend to lose that childlike love and appreciation for fun and imagination. Kids run around having fun and figuring things out, not putting too much pressure on themselves. Leadership spaces tend to be serious, strategic—with systems and structures that become static. When compared with kids, who are naturally resilient and have vast imaginations that see beyond what is actually there, who is actually more agile?

In business, just as in athletics, you have to be dynamic, willing to experiment, and quick to adapt when you see what's working and what isn't. To do all this, you must be willing to get vulnerable, lean on your team, and see beyond what's in front of you.

After the workshop, the participants took the blindfolds off and their sight was restored. But through this one exercise with a temporary limitation, they were able to see beyond many of the limitations that they thought were standing in the way of their vision.

Learn to Trust Vision over Sight

After one of these workshops, a guy came up to me and said, "That was really impactful. I've climbed mountains and gone skydiving, but running blindfolded was by far one of the hardest things I've ever done."

I asked him why that was, and he replied, "Well, you

know, when you took my sight away, it took away my ability to trust the world, but also to trust myself. My confidence was taken away because I wasn't able to see what was in front of me. Before putting on the blindfold, I could see that the track was just eight lanes. Everything is flat, and it's just a wide open space. But once I put that blindfold on, it became an obstacle field. All I could think was that I was going to trip over something, that I would hurt myself, that something bad was going to happen."

Now imagine you didn't just put on the blindfold once you were out on the track; imagine you were blindfolded before you even set foot on the track. Imagine what it's like to try to navigate this challenge without ever seeing the terrain in front of you.

This is what it feels like to be a leader. Leaders find themselves in situations where they don't know the answers; they don't know the future, and they have to take a chance without knowing the outcome. When the way you've navigated something suddenly stops working for a new challenge, how will you open your mind and find new resources?

Well, when you take away sight, you learn to develop vision. When you're anchored in your vision, you begin to expand your possibilities and recognize all the resources you can use to bring your vision to life.

A leader is someone who has the ability to see something larger than themselves. Vision expands your mind, your reach, and what you previously thought was possible. Even beyond that, it gives you an idea of where to start and how to pursue your future. Ultimately, vision is meant to transform minds, perceptions, culture, society, and the world.

The stories I'm going to share with you in this book give you the opportunity to put the blindfold on for a while, to see the world through my experiences of adapting, focusing on imagination and feeling, and determining what I can tap into, to construct this bigger world around me. I'll share lessons from running blind, how I have learned to trust others, trust myself, and ascend beyond my perceived limitations. You will see the ways I've learned to work with my blindness and you'll gain valuable insight about how to work with your own roadblocks to pursue your vision.

By looking at the world through my eyes in this way, you can learn to navigate that uncertainty and do things differently. How can you creatively come up with alternatives and use a different set of skills to achieve your goals? Discomfort doesn't mean turning around and going in the opposite direction; discomfort means continuing to push forward, through those feelings, with the understanding that you are on the cusp of doing something absolutely amazing.

But you have to trust yourself—and you have to take a risk. Navigating through that discomfort means obliterating the perceived limitations that you put in your mind, while expanding the figurative darkness that you didn't previously see.

When you break down your discomfort, breaking down your walls, barriers, and limitations, you expand light into those areas. That light is your vision. As you're able to see more, shedding more light on the path ahead, it improves your ability to be agile, to make decisions with your new understanding.

The blindfold acts as an impediment to progress. On the other side of that blindfold, you'll be able to see the world as it actually is. The road ahead is clear, and there's nothing there to stop you.

MAP WHAT YOU KNOW TO EXPLORE THE UNKNOWN

When I started speaking onstage, people naturally wanted to know about my athletic accomplishments. But after a handful of questions about competitions and medals, I inevitably got questions about my blindness.

"How did you lose your sight?"

"How did you adapt to being blind?"

It was clear from the mystified tone of voice people always used that they couldn't imagine being able to function in the world—let alone compete at elite levels—without their sight. Set in their own sense of limitation, they always wanted to know: how had I overcome?

These questions used to bug me. I was uncomfortable with the social aspects of my blindness. What did people see when they looked in my eyes? What assumptions did they make about me and my experience? I didn't like that the first thing people paid attention to was my blindness. As a result, I initially didn't welcome these questions from strangers.

Slowly, I began to realize their questions were not about blindness, but about resilience. These questions of overcoming popped up because we all experience challenges and mistakes in our lives that are difficult to rebound from. I began to realize these questions were my opportunity to make a difference in the lives of others. I could show them how I learned to see after I went blind, and my experience could teach others how to see possibility and resilience beyond the roadblocks in front of them.

The great news is, each of us naturally has the tools we need to see beyond our supposed limitations. Expanding our vision takes curiosity and imagination.

Lose Sight, Gain Imagination

At age three, I was diagnosed with a cataract in one eye and underwent the first of what would become a long string of operations to save my sight. As I healed from the first surgery, the retina in my eye detached, requiring an emergency operation. It didn't work, and after a third operation, I lost all sight in my left eye.

For the next four years, I enjoyed sight through one eye. But then, my right retina began to detach, and everything got blurry again. I endured ten additional operations on my right eye, until the doctors told my mom we were at the end of the line—I would eventually lose my sight altogether. Each day, more of the world became blurry. By age eight, I was blind.

As the world around me faded, I remember driving toy trucks around the floor of my grandmother's living room and kitchen. I had an eighteen-wheeler that I imagined transporting goods all over the country. Lines in the kitchen tile became superhighways. The legs of the couch and coffee table became distant cities. Though I was losing my sight, I filled in the blurry spaces with my imagination. On the living room floor, I saw far more than what was in front of me.

I've talked to people with sight who grew up seeing the world a certain way, and they became used to their structures, routines, and everyday sight of the environment around them. As they got older, they traded their kid-like sense of imagination for a "realistic" view of the world, and they confessed they had a hard time continuing to be creative. For every new idea, they concocted dozens of rational reasons why it couldn't become real.

Think about it: how many ideas do you shut down in yourself because your mind quickly leaps to all the reasons they won't work? What if you let yourself hang out in that space of imagination and creativity just a little longer—what might you be willing to try if you let your excitement guide you?

Imagination helps us step out of reality and out of our ordinary boundaries in the hopes of experiencing what might be possible. Because of that, imagination helps us evolve. When we're in the realm of imagination, we aren't confined by what our eyes see in the world outside, we are inspired to create something new.

Thank god for my blindness: it helps me imagine possibilities. That sense of imagination I was building on the living room floor stayed with me—and eventually became my most important tool to map and navigate the world outside.

Putting the Puzzle Back Together

I was able to see my house and my neighborhood before I went blind. The apartment where my mother and I lived was tucked into one of the corners of a rectangular-shaped apartment complex on the top of a hill. I still remember in vivid detail the sidewalk that went up our neighborhood in Crown Court, the steps up to my front door, the three-foot-high ledge I used to fling myself off of into the patch of soft grass below. I loved to do cartwheels on the lawn and to ride my bike through the neighborhood. Throughout the complex, there were five-foot-high streetlamps that lit the paths at night, and on summer evenings I would catch fireflies in their glow. There was a tree house in the back, and there were woods beyond where I would play hide and seek with my friends.

As the condition of my eyesight worsened, these details became faint and blurry. The features of my neighborhood looked more distant. I stopped running around, too afraid I might run into things. Day by day my world diminished, until one day it vanished completely. I felt like I was at ground zero. I had lost one of the important pieces of the puzzle to understanding my surroundings, and I had to use other skills and senses to figuratively "see" the space around me again.

Nothing felt familiar anymore, so I went slowly. I walked slowly and touched everything around me, trying to remember the size and position of things I used to see. I didn't want people to see my struggle, and I didn't want them to know I was blind. I was ashamed: I knew I was different, and I knew people would look at me. I wondered how my eyes looked, and whether people would treat me differently. Reluctant to stray from my front stoop, I would walk down the first few steps from our front door and sit, just touching the steps, the banister, and the leaves of the bushes on either side of the stairs.

During the healing process for my eyes, I remember feeling so timid and afraid to walk around that I was handcuffed to my mom. My mom's strength gave me courage to take small steps back out into the world. When she went to visit neighbors, I walked right beside her. At the laundromat, she gave me the job of putting quarters in the machines. I learned which machines had coin slots on the left side, and which ones had slots on the right, until I could walk up to a machine and drop in the quarters without fumbling. It was a small task, but with it came a small amount of responsibility. My mother was striking the match for independence and self-sufficiency.

Though I stayed glued to my mother's side, our walks helped me start to map my neighborhood again. I knew how many steps we went down the path before turning toward the neighbor's house, and I created a mental map of our route to the laundromat. I knew how close we were to the park by how the texture of the ground changed under my feet.

Sometimes, my mom would stop me and gently prod me to explore more. "What's beyond this point?" she would ask, and slowly her questions started to rekindle my curiosity.

I want you to understand something similar to the lesson my mom was teaching me: Although you may not be able to see what is out there, that is not the same as there being nothing there.

When you are curious—and as you want to learn more and feed that curiosity by asking questions—you expand your reach, your touch, and your knowledge. Instead of remaining in one place, stagnant, you break down walls. Curiosity shifts your mindset so that you are willing to see more than is currently in front of you. You will become aware that there may be hidden paths, if you are brave enough to explore and discover them.

People Will Doubt You, but They Don't Have Your Mindset

My mom understood my experience, because she was visually impaired, too. At eighteen, she was diagnosed with glaucoma, and she wore thick glasses. On top of her visual impairment, she was black and a woman, ticking three minority boxes while growing up in the '60s and '70s in rural North Carolina. Many of the people she'd encountered in her life treated her differently.

Still, she developed the skills and talents she needed to excel at her job in human services, and though she couldn't drive, she found a way to get to work on time each and every day. She always found a way to accomplish her goals, and she drew on her experiences to guide me.

We had to use taxis frequently to get around Raleigh, and since taxis aren't the cheapest thing on the planet, we were part of a program, Accessible Raleigh Transportation (ART), that helped make our transportation more affordable. We had a book of ART tickets we could use in taxis, and one booklet was enough for my mom to get four to five drives to work. Cab drivers didn't like the tickets, because they required the cabbies to go through an extra step to get paid. Sometimes cab drivers would simply tell my mother they didn't accept that form of payment; other times they were nasty.

My mom kept going, unscathed by the responses of the cab drivers. She would be upfront with them when we got in the cab, asking, "Are you okay with accepting ART tickets?" Occasionally, a driver would say, "Oh yeah, no problem," but most of the ones who said "okay" did so begrudgingly. Some would say "no," and then we had to get out of the taxi. She told stories of how the cab driver would put her out mid-route, and she would have to walk or get someone to pick her up, which was not as easy in the days before cell phones.

Within my young mind, I had an idea of what was going on, and I knew that wasn't right. As I began to get older and to a point where I could fully understand and comprehend more of the nuances of what was happening around me, my mom went on to teach me to respect everyone and treat people the way I'd want to be treated. She certainly didn't believe in treating someone differently just because they might have their challenges!

Every day, I saw her keep pushing forward. Her attitude was, "I have to make sure my son has everything he needs in life, and there's nothing that's going to stop me from doing that for him."

And that wasn't just talk: her whole life, my mom has modeled what it looked like to not allow anything to stop her.

The feeling of shame lingered for me, however. At school, kids would hold up their hands in front of my face and ask, "Can you see how many fingers I'm holding up?" Or they would take one look at me and say, "What's going on with your eyes?" Their questions made me feel different from them, and at the young ages of eight and nine—even ten, eleven, twelve—being different was a problem. When I experienced setbacks in those early months of navigating blind, whether I was dealing with rude comments or a cut from bumping into something, my mom was always there to fix me up, put Band-Aids on my scrapes, and gently usher me back out into the world.

"Don't allow your experiences to deter you from your dreams," she taught me. "Not everyone has your mindset; you can choose to carry on. Plenty of people will say whatever they can to knock you off your progress. Keep fighting."

I knew people would doubt me and form automatic expectations about what I could and couldn't do. But in those early years of my blindness, I had a lot of time to sit, think, and figure things out. I told myself, "Lex, sit down and determine what you need to do. Then you can plan out what tweaks and adjustments you need to make to get there."

I couldn't see my neighborhood, but I could feel what the surface of it felt like under my feet. I couldn't read print, but I could learn to read Braille. I started to get creative with different ways of doing things I loved to do.

It was only later, as an adult and a public speaker, that people began to open up to me about their own stories of shame and limitations. I recognized everyone had their strengths and weaknesses, and my own sense of shame began to dissipate.

Again, my mom was a solid example. She probably felt some of the same emotions of shame and embarrassment at times, but falling victim to those emotions wasn't going to get either of us where we needed to be in life. I learned to not ignore those emotions, that you can still push forward in life while successfully maneuvering through those feelings of discomfort.

That sense of shame feels like a "no" at times—stop doing this, don't be like that, why are you doing this—but when you understand that shame *isn't* necessarily a signal to stop, you can keep that energy moving forward. This transformation will allow you to be able to travel down the path ahead.

Vision Brings the World in Focus

After I went blind, I began to understand vision in a new way. "Seeing," to me, doesn't require eyesight so much as imagination. Blindness served up a constant challenge for me in the form of a blank slate across the world. To "see" the world around me, I needed to find or create things I could physically touch, taste, smell, or hear.

I memorized the number of paces along the paths around our house, and I learned to find my way from the bus stop to my front door. Everything was slow at first, but I began to remember how the neighborhood was laid out and I got comfortable navigating the terrain I could no longer see.

In contrast, playing with my friends was fast, and I began to push my limits by joining in on their games. I had to process all my sensory information faster when I was chasing them on the sidewalk, and when feeling my feet skip from the pavement to the grass. I needed to learn to react quickly so I wouldn't hurt myself. I wanted to be able to run at full speed, to do the things my friends could do, and to do the things I used to be able to do, like clear the three steps of stairs up to my house at a time. With practice, I learned it all, and in a game of hide and seek I raced away from my friends and cleared the steps all in one go.

As I gained the confidence to explore, I was constantly curious about what more was in my space, just out of reach. I wanted to learn every crevice and corner of my neighborhood so it would feel like home.

Once I mapped out my neighborhood, I realized there was so much more. When I reached the ends of the streets I knew, I wanted to know where the streets beyond led. There were buildings and whole neighborhoods I hadn't visited before; what were they like? Nailing down the familiarity of my own neighborhood got me wondering: what was beyond the boundaries I already knew? I started to gain confidence in the landmarks and reference points I'd established in my mind. Could I go somewhere else and navigate a new place the same way?

Blindness required me to constantly ask the question, "What can I see?" I realized there were many ways I could move around any space safely and independently to learn what was within it. I could use sounds around me to identify where I was and what might be safe to do. If I got near a park, for example, I could hear the shouts and pounding of other kids' feet in the grass. I knew there was a good chance the terrain was open in that spot, and I could confirm by asking my mom.

Vision, whether literal or figurative, is a magical process.

From nothing, you create an illustrious thing—first in your mind, and then out in the world. As I learned to understand my vision better in a very real, literal sense, I also learned important lessons about how to create the vision for my life and my career.

I learned to establish the boundaries I could play within to stretch myself. At first, my fear confined me to my front stoop. But as I mapped out the park, the laundromat, and the streets in my mind, I learned where I could and could not safely go. Over time, I built a reference library of landmarks in my mind. Once I gained a vantage point that allowed me to picture the whole neighborhood, I found myself more and more curious about what lay beyond.

That's the thing about a tantalizing vision: once you can see you're moving forward, and that you know what to do at each step, you close the distance between you and your vision until you can reach out and touch it.

Reflect on Your Own Vision

Take a few moments to journal on these questions.

What can you see? I knew what my neighborhood looked like, but I learned to see it differently—and to see more of it—when I couldn't see it with my eyes. How can you look at your roadblocks differently? How can you challenge yourself to see more? How can you continue to feed your curiosity?

How are you facing your emotions? When you experience shame, embarrassment, and doubt, do they appear as period stops? Or do they feel like commas? What more might be out there?

What can you do to push through those emotions or roadblocks and continue forward toward your vision?

What are you doing to feed other people's curiosity, to help them explore the unknown? What are you doing to help them discover and understand that just because they are not able to see what's directly ahead, that doesn't mean there isn't anything there? What can you do to help them combat that limited way of thinking?

BECOME NUMB TO "NO"

Some people have the mistaken idea that a person who is blind can't do a cartwheel.

That's ridiculous.

I did flips and cartwheels prior to losing my sight, and I did them again after; I just had to imagine the space my body was in, rather than being able to see it. I had to get comfortable doing things people didn't think I should be able to do. More importantly, I had to get comfortable doing things I knew I *could* do. I love proving people wrong, but more than that, I love proving myself right about what I'm capable of.

I built up my comfort levels slowly, starting with tuck and rolls in the living room to get used to the feeling of turning upside down without being able to see anything. After rolling over and over again, I went out to the huge patch of grass out front of our house to try a cartwheel. I knew that if I happened to lose my balance, I'd fall on soft grass.

I did one cartwheel, and eventually added another one, doing two cartwheels in a row, then three.

I thought, *If I can do three cartwheels in a row... maybe I can do a flip, too.*

Doing a front flip is a totally different experience from doing a cartwheel. You are still going upside down, but the motion is completely different. You have to follow a sequence: head down, torso tucked in just the right way, legs up in the air at just the right time.

I wasn't confident enough to just start doing a flip in one fluid motion, so I started by bending over, putting my hands on the ground, and throwing my feet into the air to do a handstand. After doing a few handstands in a row, I got a little too much momentum and flopped over on my back in the grass.

A neighbor walked by after one of these back-flip flops, while I was still lying on the ground catching my breath, and asked my mom, "Should he be doing that?"

I knew she'd heard that question more than once, from

well-meaning friends and even family members. She always responded, "He's fine. He's just being a kid."

Finally, I was ready to do the full flip. I knew that the amount of time I'd be upside down needed to be faster than I'd practiced. I told myself, "Okay, brain, get the message to my feet!"

I yelled to my mom, "Hey, Mom, look at me, look at me!"

I got more momentum, took one step forward, turned my body up, and flipped all the way over. Boom, I nailed it and landed on my feet. Perfection.

"Good job, Elexis," my mom said. "I knew you could do it."

I had to continue to grow and develop amidst this new challenge I was facing, despite the opinions people had of what I should and should not do. You also have to learn to drown out the noise. It can echo so loudly in your head that it consumes your mind and pushes out the possibilities of what you could be working toward. When that happens, you allow your distractions to talk you out of your potential. Instead, recognize that you'll likely always have noise and distraction, and you simply have to keep going.

Never Say Never

Those experiences, relearning how to flip and do a cartwheel, honed my spatial awareness. I learned how to interact in different spaces and where I fit within each environment. Most importantly, the experiences reawakened a feeling that had been very familiar to me prior to losing my sight:

I wanted to experience the satisfaction and sense of fulfillment that came from hitting a cartwheel perfectly.

At an age when I had a lot of time to figure myself out, I gravitated toward activities I'd experienced before losing my sight. I still had a burning desire to be active, to not accept the limitations other people wanted to put on me. Sports turned into my measuring stick.

There was a passageway at the entrance to the kitchen with a blank wall at the end of it. For hours I would throw a tennis ball against the wall, trying to catch it in my baseball mitt when it rebounded back to me, scrambling around to find it if I missed.

I was terrible at this game at first. The ball flew past me again and again. I listened to it bounce around the passageway, and slowly I learned to track where it was. Then I would extend my hand, and with a soft thud, the ball would land in my mitt.

Once I started catching the ball, I was elated. I hurled the tennis ball as hard as I could against the wall. The harder I threw, the faster the ball returned—but I got faster, too. I was able to catch it with a satisfying smack into my mitt.

All right, now, I thought to myself, *You're the man. You're going to get drafted in the first round and play for the Atlanta Braves. You're going to lead the franchise to a World Series title.*

As I threw the ball up into the air, I could actually *hear* the announcer: "Lex Gillette, number twelve, is at the plate. The pitcher winds up. He throws. Gillette hits the ball out of the stadium! He's running around the bags!"

In reality, I knew I wasn't going to be a baseball player. I probably wasn't going to become a basketball player, either. But I didn't actually need to be successful in a specific sport; I just wanted to recapture the feeling of playing, pushing myself, and seeing myself win.

Life is about learning, and even "pointless" activities have their purpose. It may not have seemed "important" for me to do a cartwheel—maybe the adults who doubted me even thought a cartwheel wasn't worth the risk of hurting myself. But these moments became the building blocks of new skills.

I learned to muster my courage even when I was afraid of falling. I learned to move my body through space without my sight. I learned to catch a ball by listening to the sound it made through the air.

These moments taught me that you have to learn to dig inside yourself and leverage the experiences you've already had and the skills you already possess. I already knew how to do a cartwheel and catch a ball; I was just learning to add the challenge of doing these things without sight.

Blindness became a springboard for me. I wasn't just going to do one cartwheel—when people said I shouldn't do it, I would do three cartwheels in a row. I didn't just think about being able to watch a baseball game again, *I imagined I won the World Series*. People tell me, "You might not be able to do this," but I've heard it all before and I've become numb to "no."

I knock down any opposition that comes up, just like I knocked those baseballs out of the park.

How can you learn to reframe the "no"? People often view "no" as a full stop—they believe if someone says no, it's not going to happen. But you can look at the scenario and decipher what is really being said: is this person saying "no" because they mean "not me" or "not yet"? If this isn't the right person to help you, you can continue on to find the person whose skillset does plug into this situation, who can push you forward toward your vision. Similarly, if you hear "not yet," it doesn't mean it's not going to happen, but as things are currently, you'll want to evaluate what other aspects you can work on. What other things can you assess so you can continue toward the vision?

You also have to understand that "no" isn't a no to the whole vision; you can break it down and see which part isn't going to happen, so you can find other things you can work toward to achieve the vision. By isolating the one step that's blocking you, you can find the strategies that will help you move forward. What was previously a "no" can slowly be converted to "now it's time."

My imagination took me to the World Series, but my actual vision was about being an athlete. I came from an athletic family who played baseball and softball, and I wanted to participate in sports as well. I understood that life was different for me—but that wasn't a "no."

At a time when the world was "blind" to me and my capabilities, I was able to create an experience that gave me the cheers I was seeking and the feelings of acceptance, appreciation, and worth I was yearning for. It may have looked like I was just throwing a ball against the wall, but I was also designing the world I wanted to see and feel. That's what it's all about: implanting yourself in spaces where you can see what you want to experience. I won't be in the World Series, but I might have a World Series-esque future. I can experience the achievement and energy it takes to get there, the excitement and thrill when you're down there on the field, the chills that run through your body when you make a great play. In this way, I can become one of those lucky ones who hears the crowd, hoists the trophy, and experiences the fireworks.

Wings Unclipped

In the summers when I was off school, I would take the Greyhound bus to my aunt's house in South Carolina. A long dirt road led to her house, which was surrounded by open space. I could always hear cars as they came down the road, and I felt free to run around outside, jump off the porch, and climb the trees that lined the road.

One afternoon when I was about fourteen, I heard my cousins and their friends zooming around on their bicycles. *I want to do that, too,* I thought. I hadn't gotten on a bike alone since I'd lost my sight (though I had ridden on handlebars and backs of bikes with friends). When my cousin Jamel came back toward the house, I told him I wanted to go for a ride.

"Are you sure?" Jamel asked me. He often asked me this question when I wanted to try something new. He said it with a little excitement in his voice, and I always knew he meant, "Are you ready?"

"Yes," I said firmly. "I'll follow you." I knew I'd be able to hear the sound of his tires rolling across the packed dirt, and it would be easy to stay right behind him.

"Then let's figure it out," Jamel said. "Let's go."

There are a few special people in my life who help me do things that seem wild and crazy to others. Jamel is one of them. He never let me feel like my wings were clipped just because I was blind.

The road was worn, with smooth tire tracks to the left and right, and a hump in the middle. Jamel came to the conclusion that the safest way to ride together was to stay in one of the tracks. If I went a little too far to the left or right, I would be able to feel the slight incline out of the track. The dip of the tire track would serve as a secondary navigation system. Along with listening to Jamel's bike in front of me, I felt certain I'd be able to follow.

I was incredibly excited—I wanted that feeling of freedom and balance on the bike—but I was a little nervous, too, doing another new thing for the first time without being able to see. My heart beat a little harder as I listened to Jamel ride off, and then I straddled my bike, sat down on the seat, and pushed off with my right foot on the pedal.

Whoosh, I was off! The bike rolled smoothly down the road. I felt the dirt under my tires and listened to the sound of Jamel's tires in front of me. I felt like I was on top of the world. With each cycle of the pedals, my sense of freedom and accomplishment grew. *This is really happening!*

I felt myself starting to pick up speed and shouted up to Jamel, "Let's go a little faster!"

When Jamel shouted back "okay!" I could totally hear the smile on his face, as though he was thinking, *My cousin is fearless.*

That first ride, I had a huge smile on my face the entire time. It took me back to the days when I could see. I created a layout of the dirt road in my mind, and the feeling of the dips in the road gave me a physical understanding of the track. I kept listening to Jamel's tires, to make sure I was following behind him. A couple times, I veered out of line and Jamel gave me feedback—"I'm here, cuz!"—and I made slight adjustments, turning the handlebars left or right to follow his voice.

With Jamel in front of me, I thought, *Just go for it—there's nothing to be afraid of.*

I wanted to chase that feeling of movement and speed, the bicycle propelling me forward faster and faster until I could stop pedaling and glide, feeling the wind in my face. We went down a hill, and it was exhilarating. There was a little fear in the back of my mind; I didn't know how steep the hill was or what was in front of me, but that didn't scare me enough to make me stop pedaling.

Testing the Waters

Jamel served as a conduit to elevate to different spaces—sometimes literally.

Once we mastered riding bikes down the road, we asked ourselves, "What else can we do? Where else can we go?" We built makeshift BMX ramps with cinder blocks and plywood, and I would listen to Jamel start from way back and ride fast up to them.

Doubt crept into my mind. I knew I needed to line up and ride perfectly straight, or I would crash off the ramp. There was very little margin for error.

I started closer, and approached more slowly, but when I felt the bike going up the incline, I pushed hard and launched off the ramp. The jump was a small one, but for a moment my tires were surrounded with nothing but air. I felt like Elliot in *E.T.*, riding his bike right across the sky. At least, that's what it felt like in my head.

Other times, we'd ride after torrential downpours and have to navigate around—or, more often, steer straight through—huge puddles in the dirt road. I'd hear Jamel splash through the first puddle ahead of me and I'd hesitate. He'd stop and yell back, "You okay? It's not that deep right here."

I'd keep riding, but in the back of my mind I'd wonder, *Is there going to be something big lurking unseen in the deep puddles?*" I wasn't worried about animals, but the wind during those big summer storms blew all sorts of things around. I wondered just how deep those puddles were. With Jamel as my navigator, I knew he would let me know what was ahead.

A couple of times, we unexpectedly rode through puddles so deep that my shoes and socks got wet. When we got back to my aunt's house and she saw the mud splashed up our legs, she would say, "I know y'all were out there on those bikes again!"

I didn't ask my aunt's permission to go for a ride, because I thought she might say no. After all, she wanted to send her nephew home in one piece! So I learned to not ask folks who I thought might not give me the freedom I felt on those rides with Jamel. Even if they said "no" or "don't do that" because they wanted to protect me. That was *them* feeling nervous, not me. I learned to ask people who would enable my dream—people like Jamel—and who would help me test the waters of what's possible.

I Formation

Jamel and I also loved playing video games together.

At first, I just listened while Jamel played, mostly sports games like football. I'd ask him, "What team are you going to be? Which players are you playing with?"

But then he said, "Hey, let's try something. Why don't you play, too?"

Jamel described the layout of the game on the screen. This was the early 2000s, so I only had to picture two dimensions and pretty basic graphics. He put the controller in my hand, had me feel the buttons, and told me what each button controlled. I had faint memories of games but I mostly had to rely on my imagination to navigate the football field. I wasn't sure exactly how the line of scrimmage looked (I'm still not sure I've cracked that code), but I could vaguely picture the center standing over the ball with two people on either side of him. I drew a picture of the defense in my mind, standing on the opposite side of the line, licking their chops.

We played in two-player mode, always on the same team —and I was almost always the quarterback because I could press the button to hike the ball and the quarterback on the screen would hand the ball off to the runner. Jamel would then control the runners and wide receivers, because he could see where to dodge or run or tackle people.

As I got better, I learned to hike the ball and then use the joystick to make the quarterback back up, which gave time for wide receiver routes to develop. Jamel taught me how much time each route would take, and we tried out different plays from the playbook. I memorized the different formations and what buttons to push for each—just like how a football player has to know the playbook and where the other players need to be, or how to audible out of a certain play. When we wanted to do a throwing play, a timer in my head counted down. When it got to a second and a half, I knew to press the B button to make the quarterback release the ball. While the ball was in the air, Jamel would guide the wide receiver to catch it and take it to the end zone. Touchdown!

If I stood still too long, and the quarterback got sacked, the controller would vibrate in my hand. That gave me physical feedback to go along with the images in my mind.

We often stayed up until three or four o'clock in the morning, pressing buttons and running plays. We made the playoffs and even won the Super Bowl a few times. When that happened, Jamel would describe the scene for me so I could imagine the confetti floating down and all the people jumping up and down on the sidelines.

When we played together, Jamel was helping me play but, without even realizing it, he was also teaching me how to collaborate as part of a team.

Collaboration is a muscle, and it needs to be exercised just like any other muscle. Collaborating with others helps you experience more, while also helping you expand your vision, your potential, and your understanding of what you're capable of doing. When I had my sight, I could play advanced levels of video games. But by playing in two-player mode, in collaboration with Jamel, we both learned together, grew together, and developed together.

When you collaborate and put your mind together with others, you each expand your reach and what's possible. You put yourself in the best position to see more. When I was throwing the ball against the wall, I imagined myself winning the World Series. When Jamel and I worked together, though, we won the Super Bowl—and we amplified the jubilation and exhilaration I felt when I won alone. Leaders amplify those feelings of excitement, exhilaration, hunger, and yearning for success. They also know they can't do it alone: to keep pushing things in the right direction, it's going to take partnership and collaboration.

Don't Be Afraid to Fall Over

Sometimes we're reluctant to say or do certain things because we're afraid of what might happen.

Know that people will doubt your abilities. Don't let your fear of their reactions hold you back. Ask questions, say what's on your mind, and do what aligns with your dream. Find the people who push you in the direction you want to go.

When I was doing cartwheels in the grass or riding bikes with Jamel, I wasn't afraid to say, "Hey, let's try this and see what happens. Maybe if we do it this way, it'll work."

When I tried doing a flip again, I took small steps until I was comfortable—and then I intentionally kept pushing myself. I wanted to do those same activities I'd done before I lost my sight. In my mind, nothing feels better than that sense of satisfaction, that complete and utter contentment, that comes from knowing that you did everything necessary to accomplish your goals. I *needed* to keep pushing until I achieved that. Nothing and no one was going to stand in my way.

And yeah, sometimes I fell off my bike or fell over in the middle of a flip. I scraped my elbows and cut up my knees . . . but I didn't allow that to stop me, either. My mom would put a bandage on it, give me a kiss, and send me back out into the world to keep going.

Every day we're here on the earth, people are swiping around on social media or comparing themselves to others, receiving the narrative that they have to be perfect. That's a daily challenge for a lot of us—but it's a false narrative. It's okay to be imperfect and to make mistakes. That's how we learn. If you're going to make big strides in life, you have to become okay with falling down. When you fall, you'll find yourself in a position to grow: Are you patient? Are you willing to take the time to solve this problem? Or do you easily give up?

The things that will be really satisfying, that will give you that intrinsic feeling of satisfaction in your gut—they will take some time. There will be bumps and bruises when pursuing real success and real vision.

What to Do When You Doubt Yourself

Tell yourself, "I am patient. I am diligent and courageous. I persevere. I'll successfully get over this roadblock. The scrape on my knee will heal. When I fall in the middle of this cartwheel, I'll learn from that and put in more effort until I successfully turn it—and not just one, but two, three, or even more." What becomes possible for you when you have this mindset?

Drown out the noise. When I encounter distractions and noise from doubters, it's almost insulting. Some of the questions that instantly pop into my head are: "Why don't you think I can do this? Why don't you believe in me? Why don't you think I'm the person for this task?" But instead of coming from a defensive place, I've learned to reframe my thinking: "I do believe I can do this. You're the one who has a different belief system." My mom helped me understand that only I can decide what I can do, no one else. Recognize people's doubt as doubt over a roadblock, not your whole vision.

In order to evolve, you have to tap back into what you believe. If another person's doubt triggers uncertainty in you, ask yourself, "Why can't I do that?" and identify the specific roadblock to tackle next, rather than tossing out your vision because of someone else's limited view. Instead of falling victim to someone else's expectations, shift to thinking, "I know that I can do this!"

My mom combined those words of affirmation with action: "I know you can do this, because you can... read books not with your eyes, but your hands; use a cane to get around; use text-to-speech software to navigate technology." Affirm your capability by reflecting on your past experience: What have you been able to change with roadblocks in your way? What did you do—even if that accomplishment seems small? Once we can see some level of achievement, that's the glimmer of hope we can see within the dark.

As a leader, realize that people look to you for guidance and direction; your words to your team can easily, if inadvertently, hurt, insult, or derail them. Rather than risking that, be inquisitive: ask, "Why can't this happen?" For example, if I could have been hurt doing a cartwheel, one suggestion could have been moving to the right environment to keep me safe—grass, not gravel.

Recognize people's doubt as doubt over a roadblock, not your whole vision. When you get curious about the noise, you can break it down. Put yourself in a situation where you can see more clearly, and identify what is actually going on. Once you recognize the noise, you can notice how it's similar to what you've heard before. People impose their thinking on your capabilities. When you hear doubt, that's the time to figure out how to innovate; that's your opportunity to recognize you can create change and initiate transformation. Shift your attitude to one of "let's figure out a way to make it happen," directly and indirectly showing others that this can be done.

Jamel was a leader with his question, "Do you want to try?" I may have been weighed down with doubt, but he asked if I wanted to be involved and participate, then told me, "Between the two of us, we're going to figure it out." He extended an invitation amidst a time when I didn't think I could participate, or it would be too much of a problem—and that invitation started to get my mind moving. So who can you be a Jamel to? How can you be the person to invite someone to depart from a space of doubt into a space of possibility and opportunity?

If you are the person in doubt, ask, "Can I try?" Then find the people who will help you try. We are never only in a place of needing help or only in a place of being able to give help; we are in the middle of both. Find collaborators who are willing to help you, and give back by helping others try something new.

STOP WORRYING ABOUT BLENDING IN—OR STANDING OUT

When I first lost my sight, I was told that it was crucial to use a cane to help me get around. My mom, teachers, and orientation and mobility specialists suggested I start using a cane right away, so I would use it when I was in their view, but once I was by myself I tried not to use it. When I left the house in the morning, my mom tried to get me to use the cane to get on the school bus. I didn't want anyone to see that, so once I knew I was far enough away that she couldn't see me anymore, I would fold it up and put it in my backpack, or find some way to hide it. I just wanted to avoid the questions of "what is *that*?"

By the time I was in fourth or fifth grade, though, I had to use the cane almost constantly because teachers were watching. And eventually, I had to acknowledge that it was helpful in some situations. In my hand, that cane was a tool that allowed me to navigate the neighborhood; helped me locate stairs, hallways, and doors; and warned me about obstacles on my path ahead, like trash cans or "wet floor" signs.

When I walked down the street, my cane gave me information about where fire hydrants, street lights, and stop signs were. It told me when I came to the corner of a street and enabled me to make decisions on the best way to travel. When I felt the slope of that graded plate on the sidewalk, feedback from the cane let me know that I'd reached the street corner. Then I could line myself up appropriately and walk the straightest line possible to cross to the other side of the street. Once I made it to the other side, I'd feel that same texture on the opposite corner and know I'd made it safely.

But while this tool made it easier for me to make my way through the world, it still made me feel incredibly self-conscious. I wanted to be the kid with a backpack slung over one shoulder, carrying a girl's books in my arms. I wanted to be part of the cool group of kids, so I listened to the same music—hip-hop and rap, like Snoop Dogg, Notorious B.I.G., and Usher. If you listened to anything else, you ran the risk of being picked on. "You listen to Reba McIntyre? You listen to Chopin? You're a geek!"

I wore the same shoes and the same clothes as the other kids on the bus: Nikes or Jordans; baggy jeans and jerseys or long white tees. I also watched the same shows: *Martin*, *The Fresh Prince of Bel-Air*, and *The Jamie Foxx Show*. I didn't dare to show up talking about *Seinfeld* or *Friends*!

I didn't want to stand out—especially at school. When a kid came to class wearing glasses for the first time, those glasses became their identity, the only thing anyone saw about them. I didn't want to be known as "the kid with the cane."

No matter how much I tried to fit in, when I used that cane at school, I was different, and I felt that deeply. Only old people used canes, or people who needed assistance and couldn't move around as quickly as everyone else. I didn't want to be seen as a person who had to use this slow, old person's tool; I wanted to be *cool*.

Ditching the Cane

So, in middle school, I ditched the cane. I used it a bit in sixth grade, but by seventh and eighth grades, I said, "No, I'm good. I'll figure it out myself."

Without the cane, I didn't receive the same information, so I had to take in the world around me through other methods: my hearing, the sensations I felt under my feet as I walked, and the map that expanded in my mind as I learned a new place.

I used clues I got from my ears to navigate. Teachers would often let me leave class a couple minutes early so I could get a head start before the hallways were full of other students trying to get to their next classes. Some teachers kept their doors open when they were teaching, while others kept their doors closed. I learned to listen for the voices of the teachers who kept their doors open and, by remembering where their classrooms were located, I could orient myself in the hallways. *Oh, I hear Mr. Clinton talking right now. I know I'm two doors away from my next class.*

I also used my spatial awareness to traverse the campus. When walking down a hallway, I could sense the walls on either side—without even touching them. And when that hallway connected with another, I could feel the area open up, so I knew to make the decision to turn either left or right. Stairwells were at the end of each corridor, through large double doors. As I became more familiar with my environment, I'd know whether the stairs were to the left or the right.

The first year at a new school was always the most challenging, because there was the most to learn and remember about the new environment. As a freshman in high school, I had to learn how to get from algebra class to history class, then on to English. I'd learn that specific route and fill in my mental map of the campus with the classrooms I became familiar with.

As I moved into my sophomore year, my classes were located in different areas of the school, so that added another piece to the puzzle. I had to open up the layout in my mind and fill in these new routes. In my junior year, the school was being renovated, so we moved to a different building. By senior year, we returned to the familiar campus, and even if most of my classes were in different areas, some would be familiar from the previous two years. Eventually, I just really became one with that space.

My mind had to work differently, but I was able to successfully ditch the cane because I grew more confident as I learned more about my environment and where my classes were located.

When I initially ditched the cane, it felt like a challenge. I had to tap into my other senses and my other abilities to navigate and maneuver successfully. I had to map out environments so I wouldn't hurt myself. If I ran into something, tripped over a curb, or missed a step, people would ask, "Are you okay?" But when I had the cane, people understood there was a reason for that.

When I wasn't using my cane and a janitor put up a "wet floor" sign or left a trash can on wheels in front of the bathroom, I hit those obstacles and created a scene, which was embarrassing. Kids laughed, and I imagined them pointing at me. I didn't *want* to be different, but I *was* different, and those kids made sure I knew it. I never got injured, but as I grew I realized how important the cane was to my success and well-being.

Maybe you don't want to be different; you don't want to ruin an opportunity or put yourself in a position where you're pointed at, ridiculed, looked at with the question, "Wow, what are you doing?" It's uncomfortable! That feeling of being different is overwhelming, particularly when you don't want to stand out. But if you want to be a catalyst (more on that in the next chapter), you have to be different in order to seize the opportunities to grow and evolve.

Leaders have so much responsibility placed on them, and they're viewed in a certain light. You don't want your team to go belly-up, and it can feel easier to stay in a place of comfort. But to make additional strides forward, you have to venture away from complacency into the space of the unknown.

It's not always that you're trying to keep people from looking at you; instead, it can feel like all eyes are on you and you don't want to screw up. When I compete, I walk out onto the track and I can hear that the stands are full. All these people are watching and cheering, and I have to be perfect; I can't mess this up. But how do I push past those eyes and perform at my best? I remind myself I'm here for a reason. I didn't drop into this stadium from out of the sky;

I did a lot of work to get to this point. As a leader, so did you—it took learning and working on your execution, and leveraging that new knowledge, to get to this point.

When I'm competing, I feel how strong and powerful my strides are. I think about getting my arms to do the same thing, driving my elbows back so I can get a great push. When I get to the point where I need to jump, these motions guarantee that I'll have built the right amount of speed for a big jump. That's a tool for me: those powerful, furious arms. Wesley, my guide, is my other "cane" that provides the direction. When I have him, and a great push from my start, we're going to venture into the unknown in that sandpit: it could be Paralympic records, it could be world records—the possibilities are endless.

You've gotten to this space because you are great. You are intelligent, you have what it takes, you did the work and connected with the right people, you were patient, and you trained specifically around the occupation you are in. Now that people are watching, none of that changes. Focus on the things that got you here, and hold onto that "cane" in preparation of the unknown and the new spaces you can uncover.

Be Yourself—Everyone Else Is Taken

As I got older, my understanding about the cane changed.

Back in school, I wanted to blend in with the crowd. Now, as an adult, I like to have the cane, not only because it helps me stay safe, but because it lets people know that I am blind. That indication of my blindness brings with it certain benefits: increased protection, more assistance, greater empathy. If I walk into a restaurant with my cane, people are more likely to offer to walk me to the table. Without it, though, if I just walk in and stop and wait for help, they're more likely to say, "Hey dude, what are you doing? Aren't you going to move?"

Without the cane, people assume I can see. They think I'm just like everybody else. So sometimes I *need* to stand out, to show something different about me, to get the care or assistance I may need.

But now I no longer worry about looking different or what other people will think about me. I know that *everyone* is different, and I'm good just being me.

When we're concerned with making ourselves fit in or stand apart, we're not following our true vision, one of internal satisfaction and inner peace. When we set aside the judgments of others, however, and we trust in our dreams and vision of success, we find our own path and our own rhythm.

This can be a difficult path to find—and to follow. Meeting the expectations of others often leads to conforming. It is easy to get trapped following in the footsteps of the crowd, doing what other people are doing or thinking what other people think. But you start to feel out of step. You realize you're spending so much energy trying to be like everybody else that all you're left with are feelings of pressure and anxiety. You think, *This isn't me.*

It is hard to feel out of pace with everyone around you—but you're not necessarily looking to march to the beat of your own drummer, all by yourself, either. You want to find the cadence that feels comfortable to you—that feels like the *real you*—and then come together with other people moving to a similar beat.

When you begin this quest toward what you believe success to be, your rhythm may be a little slower. As you continue to learn more about yourself, the journey you are on, and what you need to do to meet your goals, you build steam. The pace increases, and the metronome begins to tick a little faster. Eventually, you will find your rhythm and learn to make beautiful music with those around you.

Like the conductor of an orchestra, a good leader knows that every individual has their own instrument and plays their own sound. Each person may look different and have different abilities, but they are all integral to the song you want to play. The leader understands the holistic view of what is to be achieved, but they are also able to zoom in to recognize each person's strengths, to have the vision of how one person is useful in one place while another is better suited somewhere else. With that vision of how everyone's differences uniquely position them, the band finds its rhythm.

Each member can be themselves and bring who they are as an individual to contribute to the greater good of the group. With the maestro's encouragement and guidance, the band begins to play and a masterpiece takes flight.

Handle with Care

I was talking to somebody recently and they asked, "Do you ever get the sense that people treat you like you're that package that gets delivered with all those stickers all over it that say, *Fragile, please handle with care*?"

"Yeah," I replied, "all the time!"

People see me as fragile, soft, and breakable—when the reality is that I train and work out, and I'm pretty strong. They think that if I fall, I'm extra delicate and therefore likely to break something. But, in that regard at least, I'm just like everyone else: if I fall down, I'll scrape my knee. If I hit my shin on the coffee table, I might end up with a bruise. If I run into something, I might get a scar, but I'll live.

But if I get the slightest bump, people will leap to my aid, asking, "Oh my gosh, are you okay?"

That may sound like a nice thing to do, but it resonates differently when people base how to help blind people on what they've seen on TV. I've been on flights where flight attendants have offered to open up a bag of chips or can of soda for me. What about not having sight makes it impossible to pull on that little tab and crack open the soda just like anyone else? If you closed your eyes, would *you* have a hard time getting into that airline-sized pack of peanuts?

The other day, I walked out of my house in a hurry to meet up with someone, and I didn't finish tying my shoes. The lady who cleans the building flagged me down. I couldn't tell right away what she was talking about—I thought I had dropped something or my backpack was open—so I kept walking, headed outside to meet my ride. Then the lady at the front desk stopped me. "The cleaning lady saw you and wanted to let you know that your shoes are untied."

"Oh, okay," I told her. "Thanks, I appreciate you letting me know."

"I can tie them for you if you want," she said.

"No, no, I'm good. I got it."

I walked outside and almost made it to the curb when the groundskeeper, who had been Weedwacking, turned off his machine and said, "Man, I got to tie your shoes for you."

"Nah, bro, I'm good."

He didn't drop it. "Man, I can't just let you walk around like that. Let me do it."

The lady from the front desk was also there; she'd followed me out. They both wanted to just do it for me, no matter how much I told them that I was fine. I ended up stopping what I was doing, bending down, and tying my shoes—just to make them comfortable.

Had that been *any other person*, barring perhaps a small child, I don't think that encounter would have happened.

But being blind means living in a totally different world.

The worst thing is people who are so afraid of saying the wrong thing in front of me. They might start saying something like, "Hey, what are you watching on Netflix?" Then they'll interrupt themselves to say, "Oh, I'm sorry, um, what are you *listening to*?"

I don't care about that! If you say something that relates to sight, I'm not going to get upset. There are so many other things to worry about in the world. I think it's important to speak appropriately, but I'm not going to get offended by someone asking, "Did you see that movie?" That's general speech; my feelings aren't hurt by the verb "to see."

I prefer when people say, "Did you see this?" because while it may not be literally correct, it doesn't isolate me. You're not excluding me just because of a figure of speech. I feel more isolated when you say, "Did you hear this movie?"

I don't want people to forget that there are so many different meanings to expressions and how we speak. "To see" can mean to literally see, using sight, but seeing is also understanding.

People walk on eggshells making assumptions about what the experiences of others must be like, instead of *asking* about their specific experiences. When people lead with questions instead of assuming, things are a lot better. You reduce the chances of offending people, you make people feel a lot more comfortable, and you're more likely to have someone open up to you—versus assuming something, being wrong, and putting them on the defensive. I feel more open when people lead with asking questions.

Go, Tar Heels!

I am a huge fan of the North Carolina Tar Heels basketball team.

In March 2016, the Tar Heels made it to the Final Four, which was in Houston that year. I had been vacillating on whether or not to go. It was getting closer to the Paralympic trials, and I didn't want anything negative to happen as a result of attending this game.

I decided not to go, but I checked out the championship game with one of my friends who went to North Carolina and a couple other people at the Olympic Training Center. Marcus Paige, the point guard at the time, made an insane shot to tie the game with only 4.7 seconds to go. Then Villanova inbounded it and their guy shot the ball just as the horn went off. It went in. Carolina lost. We were heartbroken! I was so glad I hadn't gone to the game.

The following year, Carolina was good again. When March Madness started, I said, "If Carolina makes it to the championship game again, I'm going this time!"

They made it to the Final Four, which was in Phoenix that year—only a fifty-minute flight from San Diego, where I was training. The game and flight were expensive, so I decided to go by myself. I didn't know exactly what that would entail, but I didn't care. I booked a flight on Southwest, knowing I'd figure the rest out later.

I met some really nice people sitting in my row on the flight. One guy, who I'll call Andy, asked me, "So, what are you doing in Phoenix?"

"I'm going to the national championship game," I said.

"Oh, really? We are, too!"

"That's super dope," I said.

We ended up talking the whole flight. I could smell the alcohol from their row; drinks were flowing. They were feeling good and having a great time, and I felt like I made some new friends.

When we landed, Andy asked me, "How are you getting to the game?"

I told him, "I'm going to catch an Uber to the stadium, then I'm going to find a place to stay tonight. I have an early flight back to San Diego tomorrow morning."

"Do you want a ride?" he asked.

I thought back to when I was a kid and my mom always told me, "Don't accept rides from strangers!" But then I was like, "Forget that—I'm about to get a free ride! They seem like good people, and we're all Tar Heels fans."

I felt comfortable asking for help getting off the plane. "Hey, do you mind if I just hold on to your shoulder?"

Andy led the way out to the curbside pickup area, where his aunt was picking him up. We all piled into her huge SUV and made our way to the stadium.

When we got there, I asked, "Would you mind helping me get to the right place?"

First we had to go through security. The stadium had a rule that you couldn't go inside with an opaque bag; you had to have a clear one. I had brought a drawstring bag with me, with an extra pair of underwear, some socks, an extra shirt, and some toiletries. The security guy said, "Sir, you're going to have to take everything out of your bag."

So there I am, taking out my socks and underwear, right there in front of everybody. I knew it was nothing they hadn't seen before, but I didn't know what was going through their mind. Maybe they thought I was homeless or something! Here I am, a blind guy with a cane, carrying around his clothes and deodorant to a basketball game.

But I didn't care—I was about to go check out the Tar Heels! Security gave me a big plastic bag to put all my stuff in, and Andy helped me make my way to the right section of the stadium.

"Are you good from here?" he asked.

In my head, I thought, *Heck no! We're just standing here. Where am I supposed to go?*

But I didn't say that. I just asked him to help me find a stadium attendant, who guided me to my seat and gave me a device so I could listen to the game. I thought the listening device would be tuned into an announcer giving the play-by-play. In this facility, however, it only played the sounds of the game: the shoes squeaking down the court and the crowd screaming when someone made a basket. It was pointless!

I tried to download the ESPN radio app so I could listen to *something* to explain the game, but I couldn't. I had to piece together the entire game in my mind, based on the directions the sounds came from and whose name was called over the PA after they made a basket.

People around me probably didn't realize I was blind, because I'd hold my phone up and take photos or video clips to send to my mom and friends. *Look where I am! I'm so close to the court, I can practically* see *it!*

Carolina won, and it was so exciting to be there in person, experiencing the fun and jubilation with the whole crowd. I stuck around after the game so I wouldn't have to deal with mobs of people all trying to leave the stadium at once. As I chilled in my seat, I was able to listen to coach Roy Williams and the MVP, Joel Berry, give speeches.

Once the stadium cleared out a bit, and they were done with the remarks on the court, I found another attendant to help me out of the stadium, and then I was on my way.

That night, as I played it back in my head, I told myself, *You went to a major sporting event in the US by yourself.*

Sure, I'd had to ask people for help a little bit—and that was totally fine—but I'd had the experience of attending a championship game all on my own.

We All Get by with a Little Help

There are times where it's beneficial to blend in, but there are other times where it's even better to stand out.

When I attended that game, I needed to stand out. If I had tried to blend in and put on the facade of being able to do it all without any help, who knows what would have happened. I could have stepped wrong on those weird, steep, awkwardly spaced stairs. Because the handrail stops and starts, I could have lost my balance with nothing to hold onto, fallen, and hurt myself terribly. There are a lot of obstacles in a stadium. And even if I had navigated them perfectly, how the heck could I have even found my seat without some assistance?

I had a goal—I wanted to be in my seat at tip-off—and there were people in that stadium who could help me expedite the process and achieve that goal. I needed assistance in order to have the best experience possible, and to experience the game (almost) like everyone else in the stadium. But in order for them to know that, and to help me achieve my goal, I had to open my mouth and ask for the things I needed—even if that meant feeling vulnerable.

People can't read your mind, and they don't automatically know what you need, so it's important to ask for help. Even people who see me walking with my cane often don't know the best way to assist me, so I have learned to ask specifically for what I need. "Hey, I can't see and I'm trying to find this person. Do you see someone wearing a blue shirt and black jeans?"

Asking for help can also expedite learning. A lot of people would rather not reach out, try to figure it out themselves, and waste a ton of time in the process when the answer could have been revealed much more easily by simply asking.

You never know where that answer will show up or what form it will come in until you ask. My help came in the form of a guy who happened to be going to the same place I was—and that whole experience only went as well as it did because I didn't care about being different. I already stand out, so I might as well ask for what I need to navigate the world and be able to experience an amazing game, too.

Most importantly, ask for help because you get to have fun! You get to enjoy people, have new experiences, and achieve your goals. To go to that magnitude of game elevated everything. I've now been to a Super Bowl and a title game of March Madness. Having the courage to ask questions helped make the whole March Madness experience possible. In a situation where I felt uncertain—I wasn't sure how I would get to the stadium, or how I would get around—getting assistance expedited the process.

You don't have to run around in circles or beat your head against the wall to find an answer; you just have to ask a question or two to reach the pinnacle of your dream.

Find Your "Cane"

What makes you different?

The things that cause you to stand out can often be tools to get you out of your comfort zone, and help you navigate things you previously might have thought you couldn't do. That's what my cane does for me. What is your "cane?"

Identify the support in your life that allows you to explore new things and expand your thinking, your access, and your opportunities. Your "cane" may be a physical tool, or an internal power, or even another person. What will give you the confidence to step out and explore new and interesting spaces? That's what nurtures growth.

To identify your "cane," ask yourself: When you're in a new situation, what do you need to know? Who can help you? You might be afraid of speaking up because you're worried you won't look fit for your role if you don't have all the answers. However, when you ask questions, you can obtain information that helps you bring things into focus—like the trash cans in the hall you need to maneuver around. You will discover that your voice is just as powerful as your opportunities to change lives.

ARE YOU A CATALYST?

I started my freshman year of high school in the fall of 1999, when I was fourteen years old, and I was a little nervous. It was a brand-new environment, a bigger school than the middle school I had attended. I didn't really know anybody, so I felt weird around this bunch of new kids. And not only was I going through the awkward phase of development like most kids that age, but I was blind! How was I ever supposed to find my cool factor?

During gym class, it was easy for teachers to suggest that I sit on the sidelines because they hadn't really been exposed to someone who was blind. To prevent this from happening, I always had someone who assisted me in physical education class. In middle school, I'd had an adapted sports and recreation (PE) teacher, Mr. Crute, who helped me out.

In high school, I had Mr. Whitmer. He changed what I and my fellow students believed to be possible.

My Mentor, Mr. Whitmer

Mr. Whitmer, who would become my mentor in the world of high school sports, was a TVI—a teacher of the visually impaired. In fact, he was the head of the visually impaired program for the school, which provided resources for people who were blind or visually impaired so they could stay in the public school setting. For example, the school had a Braillist who would take the papers I wrote in Braille and transcribe them into print so my teachers could read and grade them. The Braillist would also take printed handouts from teachers, type them into a computer, and print them out on a Braille embosser so I could read homework assignments just like anyone else.

Mr. Whitmer may have been so great in the position because he had a visual impairment himself, but his visual impairment never defined him. He was just a cool guy, and he liked to crack jokes, have a good time, and keep the mood fun. From him, I learned that it was possible to be both visually impaired and independent; because he had figured out how to be successful, maybe I could, too. He always believed I could—he believed in the potential of all the kids he worked with.

The general thought among some teachers was, "This kid is blind, and we don't want him to get hurt. What if someone throws a ball in his direction? He can't see it coming, so he could get hit in the head. Then we'd have to send a note home to his mom, and it could create a bunch of problems. Why don't you just sit this one out, Lex?"

Not Mr. Whitmer, though. He challenged that thinking and said, "Why should Lex have to sit out and not participate? He's blind, but he has full function of his hands and legs. Why don't we figure out a way to involve him in the same activities the other students are doing, so he can work with them *and* break a sweat?"

He thought about how to change the activities, to adapt them so I could participate and be able to interact with my classmates. Mr. Whitmer knew that we could all learn more about teamwork by working together.

He assisted me in PE class, leading me from activity to activity, and involving me in each exercise. When everyone was shooting baskets, Mr. Whitmer led me to the free throw line, took my arms, and physically moved me through the motions of how to shoot the basketball. Then he stood under the rim of the basket and said, "Hey, let's shoot here. Shoot here!" so I knew which direction to aim. Sometimes he used my cane to tap the rim so I could get a better idea of where the basket was. When we played golf, he jingled his keys above the hole so I could orient myself and have some idea of where to putt the ball.

As the students saw that I could do the same things they could—I just had to do them differently—their mindsets shifted. They saw my potential, and they would say to me, "Hey, Lex! Come hang out with us, come play this game with us! We want you on our team, we can help you!"

Instead of feeling gawky and awkward, I felt *included*. The other kids wanted to hang out with me, and that felt good. That changed everything for me.

Mr. Whitmer never let me get away with making excuses or trying to make other people take pity on me. He had high expectations—mirroring those of my mom. I was expected to behave a certain way in my home environment, and those expectations were upheld when I went to school: I would be respectful, have good manners, and get my work done. Mr. Whitmer's standards were right in line with my mom's; they both expected me to go to every class, to show up on time, and to make sure I had all my assignments done in a timely fashion. If those expectations were not met, there would be consequences, such as lunch detention or not being allowed to participate in certain school activities.

With Mr. Whitmer's guidance, I loved going to gym class. I loved engaging with people my age and having fun, and I finally felt like I belonged. I'd been an athletic kid at an early age, but working with Mr. Whitmer solidified my passion. Though there were schools for the blind in my area, my mom kept me in public school after I lost my sight so I could maintain that connection with students who could see. The majority of the world can see, and I knew once I finished school I would need to know how to navigate, maneuver, and interact with people who could see. I learned from the other students, and I'm pretty sure they learned from me—but it all stemmed from Mr. Whitmer's tutelage.

Those of us students who were visually impaired learned what we could do when someone believed in us and saw beyond our disability. Our sighted peers learned how to assist someone who is blind or visually impaired, and—more importantly—they learned to see what was possible. We all gained a deeper understanding that even though someone has a disability or different circumstances, they can still be successful and make a life for themselves.

Mr. Whitmer exhibited inclusion, equity, and accessibility at a time when those terms weren't the buzzwords they've become in recent years. I felt like I *belonged* in that PE class, and that mindset spilled over into other areas of my life. It helped me in all my other classroom settings. It helped me in some of the extracurricular activities I was involved in. It helped me outside of school, from a social standpoint, by just being able to feel comfortable in public, having a conversation with someone.

More than anything, Mr. Whitmer's mentorship changed my self-image. I began to view myself in a better, much brighter and more confident, light.

And once I got to that vantage point, things took off.

Learn to See a Different Path

When developing a team, a leader understands that everybody has something to bring to the table. It's just a question of whether that leader puts in the time, patience, and creativity to discover each person's unique skills. As a team faces new scenarios and complex situations, a great leader determines what adaptations the team needs so everyone realizes their full potential.

First, you have to understand people's backgrounds and experiences. Take the time to connect with the people on your team, to get to know them. When people feel like those around them don't know anything about them, they don't feel like they're part of the group—and they may not see the point of participating fully in group activities. Instead, they may feel like they are back in school, forced to sit on the sidelines and watch everyone else work together.

In order to create safe spaces for people to work, particularly within companies that value diversity, equity, inclusion, and access, a leader needs to have a good pulse on the people on their team. This can include paying attention to the language you use—and the language team members use about themselves. For example, some people say, "Lex is going to the Olympics," but I'm not; I'm going to the Paralympics. That's my reality. Some athletes would hear that and think, "You're not speaking my language, you're not meeting me where I am. You don't understand *me.*"

When you take the time to get to know another person, you can also determine what adaptations may need to be made in order to help bring forward that person's full potential. Coach Whitmer was the catalyst in my life who helped me *and* others find a new path to follow so that everyone could be involved in the fun and feel as though they were making positive contributions to the group.

This has a ripple effect. You may effect change in one person's life, and as that person maneuvers through life and encounters similar situations, they will have the knowledge and understanding to be a catalyst themselves, to be in service to other people. If someone tries to take the easy way out by saying, "We don't want to let you do this activity, because we don't want any issues or anyone to get hurt," that new leader can stand up and say, "Let's find a way to make a small adaptation and alter this activity or event so that *everyone* can be part of the group."

When everyone feels included, the entire group benefits from the combination of all those special qualities possessed by each member of that group.

One common misconception is that in order to provide reasonable accommodations, there must also be a substantial financial burden to overcome. Coach Whitmer made so many small adaptations and adjustments to allow me to be able to participate in activities—and they didn't cost anything other than the time it took to come up with the new idea. When we played golf, he used the keys *that were already in his pocket* to help me locate the hole. When we shot baskets, he stood under the hoop and clanked *the cane I already possessed* against the rim.

It only takes a bit of time and effort to put on your thinking cap and figure out how to accommodate everyone; it doesn't have to cost money.

Sometimes you will also need a bit of patience to come up with those adaptations, because the answer might not always be right in front of your face. But if you really put in the time to think about it and find another way, you're going to reap the benefits. If you're struggling to think of a path forward on your own, connect with other people who might have ideas or answers. People will appreciate that you came up with an alternate path so they can be a part of the team, just like everybody else. They will recognize that you went to great lengths on their behalf. You're going to unlock another layer of each person you accommodated. Because you helped them feel good, they will want to bring it every day, put in 100 percent effort, and be their best self.

The team benefits, the people you help benefit, and *you* benefit, too.

Courage Required

Mr. Whitmer was not only my first coach, but the person who made sure my academic environment had all the resources I needed. He understood the concept of meeting a person where they are so they can achieve what's possible and see their own potential—and his different way of thinking also changed how *other people* viewed someone with a disability.

He was a catalyst for the future success of everybody around him.

Mr. Whitmer had to have the courage to be the person to galvanize those who didn't have his same vision, who couldn't easily see what is possible. Even though some people may have thought he was an oddball, he made the decision not to follow the same path everyone else was on.

When you are the first person to propose doing something new, especially when most people want to continue doing things the way they've been done, you become the lone soldier facing overwhelming force in challenging what is thought possible. You have to have the courage to say, "No, the system must be changed," to see that it *can* be changed for the better, and to not stop until the change is made. If the path hasn't been identified, *you* can be the catalyst for the change to create a new one.

Mentors like Mr. Whitmer can also help you transcend your shortcomings and expand what you previously thought was possible, so you can perpetuate your vision for what you want your life to be.

When I first lost my sight, it was like a door swung shut. When I learned how to get around in my environment and how to read Braille so I could access information, I realized the door was still there; it was just locked.

Mr. Whitmer handed me the key to the door. He saw my talent and ability, and helped me truly believe in myself, and with his help I was able to fit the key in the lock.

But it was connecting with my fellow students, making friends, and learning to adapt as a community that allowed us to turn the key together and swing the door wide open. With their support, I burst through.

Who Do You Support?

When someone asks for help, the response might be that it feels like an inconvenience, which can make that person feel like crap. Mr. Whitmer didn't make me feel that way. When you have an understanding of what's going on, it's easier to come up with creative solutions. For example, learning to play golf was not a massive problem to solve. I understood my body well enough to put the motions together; I just needed to know where the hole was, so Mr. Whitmer helped me solve that one smaller problem. His mind was always on the question, "How can we provide access?" He thought, "How can Lex be involved? We know that being included is important for his growth and health, so of course we're going to find a way."

You can find ways to make things accessible, and encourage engagement and participation in anything, with a little bit of time and thinking. I know there were times when Mr. Whitmer didn't have the answer, but his level of understanding of how to adapt things was at a point where he was unstoppable. He looked at the situation as most great teachers do. Great teachers understand that although they're teaching specifically about a math problem or how to shoot baskets, this is about life and the impact they can have on someone twenty years down the line. You have to go beyond what's happening right now and understand you're shaping your students' future success.

The next time you're working to solve a problem with someone on your team, consider how you can expand your vision to the big picture. Beyond solving the specific problem, how can you support their growth? As you engage with others, how can you look at a situation from a larger scope?

It's not just what we're doing now; it's what we're doing for the future—for community, society, and the world. What do you want them to see?

SET YOUR VISION

Every year in high school, we had to take a physical fitness test, and one of the activities we were tested on was the standing long jump.

As it turned out, I was one of the best standing jumpers in the school. At the time, I could stand in a stationary position and jump ten feet forward.

I liked doing the standing long jump, but my coach, Mr. Whitmer, encouraged me to try the running long jump. He knew that athletes did the standing long jump as a measure of explosion and power, but that I'd *really* be able to compete in the running long jump.

Mr. Whitmer walked me to the track and explained the event to me in detail. Then he guided me through the long jump area, the runway, the take-off board in the ground, and the sandpit. He explained how I would be able to jump with his guidance. He would stand in the middle of the runway and clap and yell to give me direction. I would count my strides to the end of the runway, charging toward the sound of his voice, and take off at the right point. In this way, I was able to understand the space and what he was asking me to do.

From there, Mr. Whitmer coached me to take a couple strides and a small leap into the sand. Before I started, I had so many questions running through my mind, some silly—*Is it possible that I'll jump all the way* over *the sandpit and miss it completely?*—and some more serious: *Is it going to hurt when I land in the sand? Is this even safe?*

I had to run as fast as I could and then jump at just the right time. There are so many ways to get hurt—running into something, landing wrong, twisting an ankle—and it seemed wild to imagine throwing my body through the air like that.

I was filled with fear and uncertainty, but I put my trust in Mr. Whitmer. I ran full-out as Mr. Whitmer clapped and shouted to me, helping me time the exact right moment to take the leap. I soared through the air, doubt flipping my stomach...and then I landed safely in the sand. All the doubt was replaced by excitement and a sense of achievement. *I did it...and I didn't hurt myself!*

It turns out it doesn't hurt at all to land in the sand. As I would learn later, at the bigger competitions the sand is as fine as powder, and cushions the landing even more.

It took many more attempts and a lot of trials before I got comfortable with the event, but most of my fear dissipated just by *doing* it. I succeeded in landing in the pit, and I said to myself, "Okay, well this isn't bad at all. Now I just have to figure out how to get better so I can be more competitive."

To broaden my options even further, and to help me glimpse the possibility of competing in the Paralympic Games, Mr. Whitmer flew with me from Raleigh, North Carolina, to Kalamazoo, Michigan, to attend a weeklong sports education camp during my sophomore year of high school.

Throughout the week, I participated in different track and field events, and I learned more about Paralympic sports. There were a lot of other kids like me, and we were exposed to different sports we could potentially participate in. At the end of the week, we had competitions in the events we'd focused on. Mr. Whitmer again nudged me toward the running long jump—and I won the camp competition!

During the camp I met a Paralympian who told me, "One day, you're going to be a Paralympian, and you're going to hear *your* name over the intercom at the Games!"

Now *that* sparked my interest. It was so inspiring and motivating to hear that kind of response from people who had been in that position, who were the top competitors in their field.

Mr. Whitmer and I went back to North Carolina and I joined the high school track team for my junior and senior years. His vision opened my eyes to what was possible.

Step by Step, Jump by Jump

Mr. Whitmer didn't just help me train, he was the catalyst for helping me see a vision of myself as a professional athlete. He held that end goal in mind, and then he walked me through each of the steps necessary to achieve it.

Because I couldn't see the track, I ran with a guide on the running events. This person ran beside me and literally guided me in the right direction. On the high school team, I didn't have just one person I ran with all the time; Mr. Whitmer made it a collaborative effort. He would grab different kids who were as fast as me and say, "Hey, can you run with Lex?"

We were a team, and those students were always willing to take on that responsibility with no reservations, even if it was their first time assisting someone in that fashion. People were willing to jump in and help me, and that let me see that it was so much more than just two kids running together—it was a team moving in unison.

When I first started running, I would put my right hand on my guide's shoulder and we would both run like that. It was awkward—we had to stay perfectly in step, arm strokes and footfalls hitting at exactly the same time, so we didn't get out of sync—but I didn't really know any other way of doing it.

Mr. Whitmer knew more about adaptive sports, so he gave us a shoelace or a lanyard to serve as a tether. Then we'd run side by side, each holding one end of the tether in our hands, so I had the physical feedback of the tether being loose or pulled taut. The guide running next to me would tell me what was coming up and what moves to make to go around the track.

One of my buddies in high school, Theo, was also a long jumper and a sprinter. When we ran together, I had this feeling of freedom, of someone seeing my talent and ability, which helped *me* to see my talent and ability. I could feel myself striding forward with his presence beside me, guiding me, as I used the feeling of the track under my feet and his voice in my ear to help me maneuver around that track. "Keep turning, keep turning. Okay, we're going to go straight. Keep going straight."

It was special to have someone there not only to give me directions, but to help me push toward my goal. When I finished that first run, it felt like such an achievement. No matter how large or small an accomplishment, fulfilling a goal leads to a feeling of satisfaction in your whole body.

And it left me wanting more.

We would do sprints and speed workouts on the 400m track, me tethered to my guide. In Paralympic competition, the rules grant two lanes, one for the athlete and one for the guide. But I couldn't compete in any of the high school sprint races, because the high school association would not grant me two lanes. The rules of the long jump state that a guide cannot run with the athlete in competition, but our running workouts helped me build up the speed I needed for the long jump event.

Ultimately, I made it to the United States Association of Blind Athletes (USABA) National Championships in Colorado Springs. There, Mr. Whitmer continued to teach me how things operated and how *I* would have to operate if I wanted to continue taking it to the next level.

He helped me understand that I had to be in the right place at call time, when the PA announcer came on and said, "All the men's long jumpers report to the call tent." He made sure I was there so I could compete with everyone else, and not get removed for being late. He helped me pin the bib with my number on it to my jersey. Most importantly, he helped me with my mindset, reminding me of what we had practiced and that this was just an extension of all my training.

Mr. Whitmer told me, "This is what you have to do if you want to be successful and continue getting to the next stages. You're not going to have any leeway in terms of showing up late for the call time or having the wrong spikes in your shoes. In the larger competitions, they're going to expect you to know those things, expect you to follow those rules—and if you don't, you're going to be penalized. We're doing this to get to the next competition, to get to the Games, to win gold medals. You don't want to jeopardize any of that because of negligence or not knowing what to do. You've gotta be responsible, Lex. You can *do* this."

His words made me want to continue running toward that future he saw for me.

Picture What's Possible *Beyond* What You Can See

Mr. Whitmer helped me paint a picture of how this event, the running long jump, could shape my life. Through the platform of athletics, I could compete in bigger events, travel the world—even share the lessons of my own vision on stage.

Setting a vision requires leaders to picture what's possible *beyond* what they can currently see. But sometimes accomplishing that vision means first learning to accept help when it's offered, to use every tool in the box.

I had to understand that Mr. Whitmer was there to help me and then leverage that help and all the knowledge he could give me, because it would have been difficult—if not impossible—for me to participate in this event successfully by myself. I had to trust Coach Whitmer, work with him, and follow his lead.

A catalyst can't be a catalyst unless the person they're helping (their mentee) wants to receive that help. Without that most important piece, the leader's power and impact are reduced.

Sometimes, the mentee adopts a similar vision as their mentor. Within that discovery, the mentee may see, "Oh, man, this is me. I love this; I want to go after this!"

But there are also times when the mentee has a certain vision or certain aspirations for themselves. Then the mentor has to see their vision as well, so the mentor can show the mentee how to get there.

Really good mentors, catalysts, understand that in order to see more, they may have to adopt parts of somebody else's vision and point of view. When they step into that space, the mentor expands their overall visual acuity as well.

Mr. Whitmer possessed that talent. He helped us create our own visions, then equipped us with the set of tools we would need to get to those visions.

His vision was of a classroom where everyone could participate and a future where all students were able to see their own strengths and possibilities. And he had to be creative and adaptable to find the right strategies to get to that place. There were a lot of different paths to get there, so he experimented with what tools would work best.

Most importantly, Mr. Whitmer understood that he worked with a demographic whom society told "no" more times than "yes." Society saw us as needing more help than other people, and questioned our abilities. Mr. Whitmer recognized that and refused to allow us to adopt that mindset or fall victim to that way of thinking. He made it his mission to do what was necessary so we could be successful members of society.

Mr. Whitmer wanted absolutely everyone, disability or no disability, to have the mindset of being a victor, of being able to go out and achieve whatever they want in life.

Tap into your imagination and picture the possibilities. What do you want to do? Create an outlook for what the future can be. Once you've set your vision, you have something you can work toward, and then you can get clear on what you still need. You'll be able to see who to connect to, which skills you need, and whose skills you can lean on.

You decide who it is you want to become; no one else makes that choice. Refuse to be confined to other people's expectations. Instead, look at yourself as someone who is capable; who is a victor; who can succeed at all costs, despite all circumstances. When you can shift your view of yourself to one of a champion, it helps you see yourself in a better light, with a better self-image. Deep down inside, you will find the motivation to continue pushing forward, despite what may be happening externally.

Don't limit your vision to what you currently understand yourself to be capable of; you can find people in your network to fill in the skills you need to accomplish your vision. My mom recently went to a conference, and I gave her a goal to meet two new people a day. It's important to meet new people and learn about others; you might find that the person you meet has a skillset that can help your vision evolve.

Similarly, allow yourself to be a Mr. Whitmer; become that resource to help others with their vision. Recognize that they have something uniquely special to offer to your vision and to the world.

A Flying Leap

In 2004, as I was finishing my freshman year of college, I earned my spot on the US Paralympic team. By then, Mr. Whitmer and his family had moved hundreds of miles away to Georgia, but he still made the drive back to Raleigh to help me compete and secure a spot in the Paralympics.

I was so excited. Just one year earlier, I had graduated from Athens Drive High School—and now I was going to get to go to Athens, *Greece*! I was nineteen years old, and that was my first flight across the ocean.

I just had to find someone to be my guide. Mr Whitmer would have done it, even though it would have meant being away from his family for weeks; that's just the type of person he is. But a fellow athlete at the Olympic Training Center knew someone who was a good fit: another athlete who had just missed the Olympic Games in the 100 meters, and who lived and trained at the Olympic Training Center.

That's when I met Jerome.

I went out for a week and a half to California, to a pre-Games training camp at the Olympic Training Center. I felt like a fish out of water in this unfamiliar area that I couldn't see and hadn't learned to navigate. I never learned the whole complex; I just learned the places I needed to go, like the cafeteria, sports med, and the track. After the training camp, I returned home for a few more weeks until it was time to head out for Athens. Then Jerome and I had one more week in Greece to work out our partnership before game time.

In total, Jerome and I had about two and a half weeks to train together, to learn to work with a new person, and for me to put my trust 100 percent in his hands. We did our best, but it was a demanding environment with a lot of pressure on both of us.

Finally, it was time for the Games.

In my very first Paralympic Games, just as we'd trained, Jerome stood in the middle of the runway and clapped so I knew where he was and where to go. I heard his voice coming closer and closer. Once I got really close, he moved out of the way so I could jump.

At least that's what was supposed to happen.

For some reason—maybe he didn't expect me to pick up that much speed down the runway; maybe he just froze up—he didn't move out of the way fast enough, so I clipped him, and the momentum sent me tumbling into the long jump pit.

It was completely unexpected—for both of us.

For a moment, I was lying in the sand, stunned and numb. When my feelings resurfaced, the first emotion to pop up was embarrassment. That morphed into a shocked disbelief.

I can't believe that just happened to me!

Finally, I was worried. I had twisted my ankle when I fell, and I wasn't sure what would happen when I stood up. Would I be okay? Was I going to have to leave and not be able to compete, after working so hard to get here?

I stood up slowly, brushing the sand from my legs, feeling throughout my body to see if I was hurt. Fortunately, I was fine.

Jerome was beside me, making sure I was okay, too. Then he said, "Do you hear that, man?"

I listened. The crowd was clapping and whistling. "That's all for you, bro," Jerome said. "They came to see you jump!"

My ears perked up and my eyebrows raised. "Really?"

I had been marginally aware of the crowd, but only as background noise. There was so much going on and, after all, they could have been cheering for someone else, for a different event entirely.

No, they were cheering for me.

Bolstered by their encouragement—and Jerome's unwavering support—I picked myself up and went on to compete again. The second jump earned me the silver medal: I made it to the podium!

The Difference between Pitfall and Podium Is in How You React

Fortunately, what happened with Jerome didn't turn into a bigger situation. Having someone there solely to help me achieve my goals—someone who helped me and who believed in my potential—outweighed any anger that may have been on the boil within me.

I asked myself, *If the situation* had *turned out differently —if I had twisted my ankle and not been able to go on to compete in the event that led to me taking the podium— would my outlook have been different?*

I would have been bummed out, that's for sure. Jerome likely would have felt disappointed—and maybe guilty as well. But at the end of the day, would that have deterred me from lining up on the runway with him again?

No.

I trusted Jerome, and that's the most important quality to have with a guide. It's extremely difficult to find guides. In the long jump, you want to be paired with someone who is going to provide the best audible cues possible. This is what gives an athlete who is blind the confidence to know exactly where to run and jump from. You also want your guide to keep you safe. If I veer too far to the left or right, I need my guide to make the proper adjustments so I'll run and take off from the correct spot. If I veer too far off course, I need my guide to yell "stop" to eliminate any potential collisions with cameras or any other obstacles that might be in the area.

When we're on the track, the guide has to be fast—but they also have to learn to run at the athlete's pace. The athlete dictates the race speed, and the guide guides them around the track. The guide has to be loud and provide great directional skills because they are acting as a literal *guide* for someone who can't see anything.

Beyond being able to get great results on the track, we need to vibe, to match on deeper levels, so we can create the type of relationship where, in these hard practices, in these high-pressure situations, in these highly competitive competitions, I know I can suit up and trust my guide 100 percent, at all costs. And they're there for me by any means necessary, in service of the dream I have.

Over the course of my career, observing other athletes working with guides, I've been around guides who have had great individual performances, running a low ten-second time in the 100 meters, but who viewed being a guide runner as their opportunity to train at the Olympic Training Center, to use the time to work on their own aspirations—and not the aspirations of the athlete.

Jerome, on the other hand, was there for *me.* He had to learn a completely new way of assisting someone else, and continue to operate at that high level—and he had to adjust to it all within two and a half weeks. He wasn't there because of what was going on in the stadium; he was a vessel to help me transport myself to the next level.

When mistakes are made, it's easy to get frustrated or blame others. But leaders can step back and remember that the people they work with are there to help everyone achieve success together.

When setbacks happen, it's important not to make impulsive decisions stemming from an overwhelming emotion. Any emotion can take over—irritation, anger, sorrow, even extreme happiness or excitement. Instead, find the middle ground, find your center, so you can look at the situation with a clear set of eyes. When you can gain that clarity, you'll see the setbacks are simply accidents or mistakes. Setbacks don't mean all is lost; they're just part of the growth and development, part of our journey toward our vision. We have to have a few bumps and bruises so we know what not to do moving forward, and we can make the necessary adjustments so that type of situation doesn't happen again.

That clear vision will also help you appreciate the people who are there to elevate you to a new space. In order to excel and keep pushing forward despite challenges and mistakes, we need the people around us and their skills and talents to drive the vision forward. If a leader can firmly stand in their center and recognize they can't do it without their team, it makes it a little easier to maneuver down the path of success. Approach setbacks with your team from an attitude of "Let's figure out what happened and what needs to change so we can keep pressing down this path, because I can't do this without you."

The Magic of Vision

Vision is a magical process.

Mr. Whitmer helped me dream bigger than I ever thought possible. And, at first, that's all it was: a dream. It wasn't physical or tangible, something that I could hold in my hand. It was just a picture in my mind.

But I was able to *see* it. With help from Mr. Whitmer, Jerome, and all my other teammates and athletes, I was able to believe in that vision so much that I could develop a plan and determine the necessary steps to accomplish it. I connected with the right people to help me see what was possible, people who provided resources and words of encouragement.

Ultimately, you will begin to see that vision unfold and become a reality. It becomes physical, tangible. It becomes possible.

And, eventually, you begin to see *beyond* the vision you first held in your mind. You see that the path continues past "the end," and you are able to live out the dreams you could hardly imagine when you first set out.

For me, it started with just two people out there on that track in Raleigh, me and Mr. Whitmer, trying to make it happen. Next thing you know, all that work and everything we were doing in the weight room and on the track helped to spark the nomination to that first Paralympic Games. I started traveling and winning medals. And then I went beyond what we originally thought was possible: being invited to the White House to meet the Obamas and the Bushes. Being sponsored by Nike. Speaking in front of the Brooklyn Nets, Chicago Bulls, and Los Angeles Chargers.

Even as I'm living it, it's still wild to think about. And now I get to focus on how to use all the things I have achieved to find more success, to leverage my achievements into doing more good in this world.

Once you get a taste of that magic, you won't be able to stop turning small sparks into flames that burn for something *more*.

Who Do You Want to Become?

What is it you want to do? Who do you want to become? What do you see yourself achieving, for you and for the world?

So often people let their own perceived obstacles and challenges stand in the way of what they think is possible for themselves. But I gravitate toward the things I wanted to achieve, using that feeling of satisfaction, of feeling deep down in my gut that I won, as motivation.

You have to understand that you are able, that you have something uniquely special to offer. Look at the times in your life you were successful, when you achieved something—it doesn't matter how big or small it is. Look at those places you overcame something. Then ask yourself, "What more can I do? How can I use the skills I used to accomplish this goal to achieve even more?" The "even more" points to your vision, the one thing hanging in the balance that you begin to see you could potentially achieve, no matter what the rest of the world says.

You might be someone who knows their vision right from the jump, or you may need a little kick-start. Seeing yourself accomplish something opens the door to a larger vision. Figure out what it is you've done to this point, and use that as the fuel to the fire that helps you see yourself doing some really massive things.

Then commit to it. Put all your energy into it. You're doing a disservice to yourself and others if you're only playing around. This is serious business; vision has the ability to transform minds, transform society, and transform the world. Connect your entire being to your vision.

You don't have to do it alone, and you can't do it alone: you're going to need assistance from others, and you'll need to make contributions to others as well. Look to collaborate with others who have specific characteristics that will help you begin to unfold your vision.

Now put some action behind it. How can you use your skillset to bring that vision to fruition? How can you use your talents to assist someone else in achieving their dream? Mr. Whitmer contributed to my aspirations, but he was achieving his own vision—putting students in the best position to succeed, within sport and within life. He helped me see my goal and fuel it, and it ultimately circled back to his own vision, which was to empower his students, to help them see they don't have to be victims of the world and the misconceptions it tends to have for people with a disability.

When you contribute your time, your skillset, your talent, and your abilities to another person, it helps to expand your vision, allowing you to see how your participation in one area can help you in your own pursuits.

VULNERABILITY IS THE KEY TO EFFECTIVE TEAMWORK

After college, I decided to move to San Diego to be at the Olympic Training Center full-time. I'd been traveling from my home in North Carolina to Chula Vista (near San Diego) to work with Jerome, and we met up at periodic training camps to ensure our bond stayed strong for competition. In between camps, while I was at college in North Carolina, Jerome worked with other athletes who lived in Chula Vista. When I graduated and decided to move to California, I didn't want to interfere with the relationships Jerome had built with athletes there. The relationship between an athlete and their guide is unique and complex, built on a wide range of factors that can take time to develop. We decided to find another guide to work with me full-time.

I met Wesley when I came out to the Olympic Training Center for a track and field development camp in 2007, when I was still in college. Jerome introduced me; he and Wesley had grown up together. When we started working together after I graduated and moved to the OTC full-time, it felt like we were friends who just hadn't seen each other in a while, like we were getting reacquainted—Wesley has that type of personality. It was like catching up with a friend—one who just so happened to be very familiar with track and field. It's a big plus to find someone so involved with the sport.

From there, we had to get comfortable working together. I had a decent understanding of how to help someone feel comfortable working with a blind athlete. I wanted him to feel like he had the freedom to do his job. Given that it was his first time in this position, I knew there may be some situations that he didn't know about, so I would have to explain better ways that I can be assisted. Sometimes people have good intentions but they *over* help, which can be offensive, making me feel like, "Oh man, you didn't think I could do that on my own? I can cut my own steak!" (Wesley didn't do *that*, though.)

In new situations, we have to be empathetic and understanding. We need patience, and we need to be open and honest about what helps and what doesn't, what we find irritating or frustrating, even what we find offensive. We must explain as much as possible so the person we're working with understands our triggers as well as what motivates and inspires us.

Wesley and I definitely had a learning curve. I was only twenty-two years old, but I knew the basics of running on the track and what was helpful, so I was able to tell him what I'd learned, what I was used to hearing when I was on the track, what I was focusing on. It was important for me to give him the playbook, to open the door to him, so he could take it all in—inhale and absorb everything—which expedited the learning process.

Wesley had never guided people before, so the only way to get that process going in the right direction was to be vocal and tell him, "Hey, here's what is most helpful for me."

Sharpening Our Communication

The first step in developing my relationship with Wesley was getting really impactful, clear communication. To do that, I had to be vulnerable enough to tell him what I needed from him and what my experience was like. Then we could both start to see the world through each other's worldviews and experiences, to understand what was going to be most impactful.

Initially, when I was running in sprint races, Wesley would give me very positive feedback as we made our way around the track: "You're doing good. You're doing good, keep it straight. Pick it up, pick up more speed. Okay, doing good."

As an athlete, that was good feedback; it was positive, and it let me know that I was doing something right, that I was moving fast and things were going well. But as our relationship evolved, Wesley became even more descriptive in how he explained what was going on on the track, which is more effective for an athlete who is blind.

When I was running the curve portion of the 200 meters, he used to say, "Okay, good, good, good. Right there!" That evolved to saying things like, "Okay, keep going in, in, in," to indicate that I had to veer to my left on the curve of the track so I could run it properly.

As our communication evolved and expanded during races, where previously it might have been, "Come on, we're almost there," now he incorporates specific race markers. He'll call off the sixty-meter mark, the eighty, the ninety, and he lets me know when to lean as we're coming in to the finish. He delivers concise pieces of information as fast as possible while we're running—short commands that serve as markers to let me know exactly what I need to do in the race.

Wesley has developed the skill to understand what cues will help me the most. To someone who is blind, it's not useful to say things like "your water bottle is over there" or "your shoes are behind you." A more helpful direction sounds like, "Lex, if you take one step to your right and reach directly in front of you, you'll feel your water bottle," or, "Lex, if you reach your left hand behind you, you'll feel your running shoes." The extra description and the words Wesley uses on the track bring the race into vivid image for me. As I imagine myself running it, I can almost see what I'm doing, which sets me up for a better race.

So much of the connection between us relies on trust. Better communication leads to a stronger sense of trust, which increases my confidence—and the speed I can go. When you're working with someone else, at the highest level of competition, in huge stadiums full of thousands of people, with adrenaline running high, the energy almost doubles. The natural talent it takes to get to the Paralympic Games, coupled with the performance boost of adrenaline *and* a guide to give really great information and directions—that makes you feel more comfortable and lets you know that you can succeed.

While Wesley and I had to build that trust between us, you are likely going to have to build trust between yourself and whoever you're bringing along on your vision.

Find ways to improve communication so it can be more impactful. It will resonate differently for this person because it gives them permission to hit another gear that they may not have been able to hit without that increased communication. Offer that communication, not only so they can level up, but also so they know they can trust you. They know that you will give them the tools, words, guidance, communication, and direction they need to get to that next level.

And that goes both ways—they give you the tools, guidance, and direction right back. It's very much a co-creation. It's like an incubator. You give them something, and they put it in the machine and give it the right attention and action so it comes out bigger and better, with more life, stability, and confidence. With the two of you working together, your efforts create a total transformation.

Feedback to Fly

Now, more often than not, even when Wesley and I are competing, it feels like training in many ways. Everything internally happens more slowly because we have locked in that understanding of what we need to do. It feels organic, cool, fun, and stress-free. Of course, I feel some of the natural pressure from competition, but most athletes feel and can juggle that. I am free of the stresses from being unprepared. We have everything in place, which allows me to just listen to Wes's voice, run as fast as possible, and jump farther.

As Wesley and I have deepened our partnership over the years, we've refined the ways Wesley supports me during events. I go into every competition with a clear vision of what I need to do to succeed, but Wesley has learned every possible detail of the sport, so that he can be my eyes when we walk into the stadium. He even obtained his level one and level two coaching certifications in order to gain knowledge about the sport, the events, the techniques, and what it takes for athletes to become better.

Although he may not be my primary coach, strengthening his knowledge of the sport from a technical aspect definitely provides benefits to me when I'm out there competing. Wesley can say, "Okay, I can see that you're doing *this*, that *this* is happening. Don't forget to keep your chest up, make sure you keep your hips under you." Those technique tips help me have some really good jumps and races.

I've recognized that some other athletes are so dependent upon their coach that it almost becomes a disadvantage. If that person isn't there, they don't know exactly what needs to be done, the steps to be followed to perform well. When your connection and ties to that person are that strong, it can impact your confidence and performance. That becomes its own challenge, and it's not the best mindset to have when you're on a huge stage for a competition.

That pitfall became one of the things I wanted to eliminate. Don't get me wrong, I love having my coach there. I love to have that support—it is very useful and necessary—but if for some reason he can't be there, I still want to have that confidence and trust in myself, in Wes, and in our ability to collaborate and still get the job done.

Equip yourself with the right tools so you can still perform regardless of who else is around. Whether your boss, your mentor, or your teammate is near—whoever you look to, to help set the path of what you need to do—I want you to realize that you can still do this. Take responsibility for your vision and the path you are on so that you can continue to steer the ship even when the moving parts move, when that person is gone, or when your resources change.

That guide, mentor, or boss gives you solid direction. They empower and motivate you, equipping you with the right tools and skills. But at some point, they have to step aside and allow you to take the helm. If you watch me compete, you'll see that at a certain point in the approach, Wesley moves out of the way and allows me to take those last few steps and jump forward. If he doesn't step aside, we could collide, which could leave me with a failed attempt.

I want you to have the confidence to know that it's fine

when your mentor steps aside. They've helped you as much as they can, and gotten you as far as they are able, and now it's time for you to continue to move forward. There's still work to be done—you have to take those last couple steps on your own so you can take that leap and soar into your destiny.

If you are the mentor, understand that you can't continue to stand there, because that will impede their progress. At some point, you have to let the person you are helping soar and fly. You've given them the best directions possible, and you've empowered them in a phenomenally impactful way. Trust that when you step aside, they'll have the confidence to keep blazing the trail and leaping into their dreams.

It's Personal

The relationship that Wesley and I have built *off* the track helps strengthen what we do *on* the track as well. We grab food together, and we talk about albums, shows, or current events. The more our connection grows, the better our communication becomes on the track.

After years of working together, I have a deeper understanding of his personality. We share personal anecdotes and offer suggestions or guidance if we run into any issues in other areas of our lives.

We have been able to unravel another layer of the onion, to understand each other so we can anticipate how each of us might think or feel in different high-pressure situations. When we are in those moments, I can think back to the information he's given me regarding prior experiences, to have an idea of how to navigate the situation so he feels comfortable, so he doesn't feel stressed. I can use things he might have told me in the past to help alleviate what he is currently going through.

When we warm up, we typically spend forty to forty-five minutes jogging laps and doing drills. Even though we spend a lot of time together off the track, those warm-ups are our "Dr. Phil" time, where we talk about what we have going on in our lives, professionally and personally.

As our communication has evolved, it's become more impactful, which has led to increased trust. Learning more about Wesley as a person has helped to open the door to even more progress and potential on the field of play, which is huge.

When you continue to evolve your relationship, to the point where you're able to share more about yourself, it unlocks greater potential between you and your partner, group, or team. Sharing openly doesn't just give us more information about each other, it builds trust and motivates each person to build responsibility within the relationship. When we have vulnerability in our relationships, we open ourselves up to more insights. Vulnerability can help us get to a different space, a higher level, where each of us can be our true, authentic selves.

What Does Your Authentic Communication Look Like?

Your ability to be vulnerable and to communicate honestly impacts your ability to collaborate with others. In addition, you have to empathize with the person you're communicating with, so you understand how your communication is being received. Take a moment to reflect on your own ways of communicating.

What can you do to improve your communication so it gives another person confidence and boosts their comfort, so they can achieve their goals? What do you notice about your communication so that it can evolve?

If someone asks you a question and you think you already covered that topic, they're probably not asking because they didn't hear you; it's probably because there's some element they didn't understand, even if they haven't identified that yet. Pause and consider how you communicated initially and compare that to how you can communicate the answer in a different way for their increased understanding. Take an inventory of yourself: What needs do you have that you can talk more about? How can you be more vivid in your descriptions, so you can give more clarity on how to create the outcome you want?

I have to have trust between me and my guide. What does trust look like within your environment? When is a time that trust has been broken? How were you able to mend it again?

WHO FUELS YOUR VISION?

Whenever anybody has told me that I can't do something, I immediately think, *You must not know me very well!*

Take driving, for instance. I was always told that I'd never be able to drive a car...but, with the help of my college roommate, I did just that.

Some people may wonder *why* I would even want to try doing something I'd never be able to do on my own. Well, I wanted to at least try those things that everybody else gets to do. I wanted to have that experience, especially as a nineteen or twenty year old. At that age, in that time in society, the guy was expected to pick up the girl to take her out on a date. I'll never be able to do that (although, of course, in today's world I can just send a car to pick her up), but I still wanted to know what it felt like.

So one day, after Josh and I had been friends and roommates for a couple of years, I said, "Hey man, let me drive your car."

"I don't know about that," he replied.

I pushed him a little bit. "C'mon, man. We can find an empty parking lot and you can give me some audible cues: let me know when to turn left or right, when I need to give it gas or push the brakes."

He chuckled. We were always joking around, and he assumed this was another joke.

"I'm serious. I want to drive a car."

"No, man," he said, "we can't do that." He tried to change the subject. "What do you want to eat tonight?"

But I wouldn't let it die. "Come on, man! Come on, let's go!" I begged.

He thought about it for a minute, then finally said, "Okay, let's do it."

We intentionally waited until later in the evening when parking lots would be emptier. My roommates always kept the keys hanging on hooks just inside the door, and I heard the jingle as he lifted keys off the peg. My stomach flipped with excitement. When we stepped out of the apartment to the parking lot, he led me not to his car, but to his girlfriend's.

"It's an automatic," he said, but I wondered if his real plan was to spare his own car from any mishaps. "You couldn't possibly think we'd take my car," he added. Fortunately, us borrowing her car didn't ruin their relationship. They're happily married with three kids.

He drove us to a big, open parking lot and parked the car. We switched sides, and I hopped in the driver's seat. For just a moment, I sat there, overwhelmed with excitement. *This is insane. I'm* behind the wheel *right now!*

Josh showed me the gas pedal on the left and the brake on the right. "Okay, you have to put it into drive," he said, and he showed me how many clicks to move the shifter down. Then he said, "All right, it's time to go."

I had my foot on the brake, and I let it go, expecting the car to start moving. Josh said, "You have to push your foot into the gas pedal a little bit."

I did as he told me, and the car jolted a little forward. *Aw, man, this is magical!*

We were still moving super slowly, so Josh said, "Alright, you can give it a little more juice."

I pressed down on the accelerator a little more, and the car started to accelerate a bit. I didn't press the pedal very hard; I didn't want to ruin Josh's girlfriend's car, or jump up on the curb and run into something, or worse, someone.

"Alright, you can put a little more mustard on it," Josh joked, and I pressed the gas some more. My excitement built from 100 percent to 1,000 percent! It was so thrilling, but it was frightening as well. I literally couldn't see what was going on. Sure, Josh was there to tell me what to do, but I couldn't see through the windshield to make sure we were going the right way.

Then Josh said, "Get ready. When I count down and get to one, I want you to begin turning the steering wheel to the right. Ready? Keep straight, straight, straight, and five . . . four . . . three . . . two . . . one . . . *boom*. To the right, to the right, to the right. Okay, good. Straighten out. Turn it back to your left a little bit. There you go, hold it straight."

I had done it—I had turned the car. I was driving, and I couldn't believe how awesome it felt!

As I listened to his instructions, my uncertainty drifted away. I felt empowered holding my hands on the steering wheel and feeling my fingers resting in the indentations, knowing that I controlled where we went and how fast. I flashed back to myself as a kid, rolling trucks across the floor, and wondered what that kid would think if he knew that someday he'd get to experience that for himself. *Man, this is everything!*

Josh said, "Okay, we're at the opposite end of the parking lot now. Let's give it some more gas."

I drove faster, moving forward until he instructed me to turn again at the other end. I don't know how long we were out there, just driving from one end of that parking lot to the other, but I had the biggest smile on my face the entire time.

Like my cousin Jamel, who encouraged me to get out there and ride my bike with him, Josh is one of those people who allowed me to push the limits and blow past any boundaries placed on me. I mean, I was completely blind and *I was driving*. There's no way the DMV would have allowed me to get a license, but who cares. At that moment, it didn't matter.

Josh helped me see that, even away from the long jump pit, I could still fly.

See Past Your Limitations

Josh made me forget that I was blind.

When you have a connection like that with someone, they help you see past your so-called limitations and forget about any "weaknesses" or perceived shortcomings. That collaboration helped me achieve a task I would not have been able to do on my own.

This is important for emerging leaders and leaders of newly formed teams to remember: when someone is in a new environment, surrounded by new people, they might find all that newness daunting and be tempted to count themselves out. They see themselves as being small and easily intimidated. But if they are able to find even one person to connect with—whether it's because that person has a more outgoing personality, they're more empathetic, or they just vibe—that relationship can help the new person feel like it's no big deal. With someone else in their corner, they can work around their fear, and put their mind together with the other person to figure out how to get things done.

As a leader, you have the opportunity to meet people where they are. Take the time to understand the members of your team and their capabilities, and look for the potential in those team members. Make sure your team feels supported, but push them to be their best as well. Together, you can achieve even more.

When a person or society tells you that you can't do something, ask why. Obviously I knew why I couldn't just hop in the car and drive away, but why couldn't I have an opportunity to get behind the wheel?

For leaders, that question—why not?—is very important. Instead of accepting at face value that someone can't do something because there's a rule against it, see if you can help them maneuver toward "I *can* do this." Leaders move mountains when they have a similar way of thinking as my buddy Josh.

So how can *you* live like a Josh? What can you do to interact with somebody like that? How can you give someone that freedom to see what they can do, where they can go, and who they can become? How can you learn to understand when to give that person a slight nudge, to tell them to press on the gas a little harder? They may not be comfortable, and they might not be able to see the terrain in front of them, but with your perspective, they know that they are protected and being guided to the right place. A mentor's ability to share a potential vision for the future can help someone move beyond those supposedly unsurpassable obstacles.

What do you need to do to become the person who can help somebody maneuver from their starting point to their destination?

Envisioning a Career

When I was in high school, my plan was to graduate, go to college, and get a degree. I knew that I would have a shorter shelf life in athletics than in the workspace; it was important that I have an education so that if sports didn't work out or if I were to get some sort of crazy, career-ending injury, I would have something to fall back on. I didn't want to be the person who falls into the routine of following the same pattern every day, always knowing what to do, and then suddenly being thrust into a new space and being completely in the dark as I flail about trying to figure out my next move. Getting my degree would give me a safety net.

I graduated from college with a degree in recreation management, which exposed me to so many interpersonal skills useful in sports and recreation, and to understanding what we could learn from participating in a sport. In the program, we learned how to work better as a team, find better strategies to achieve our personal and professional goals, and grow both interpersonal and intrapersonal competencies in ways that were previously uncomfortable. Athletics, sport, and recreation were used as a conduit to educate us about how to become better people and professionals.

One time, we went hiking for a weekend at one of the national parks in North Carolina. This wasn't car camping, where you drive to the campground and have bathrooms with toilets and showers. First, we had to learn about internal-frame and external-frame backpacks, how to pack them properly, what foods were best to pack, and how to cook without having a stovetop or oven. Then our camping professor dropped us off at the entrance to the park, and we had to hike for a few miles through the woods to find the actual campsite.

On our hike, we came across a stream that wasn't as big as a river but still too big to run and jump over. We'd have to cross it by stepping on rocks that spanned the width of it. My classmates positioned themselves around me to help me cross.

"Okay, Lex, before you step forward, I just want you

to listen to me describe what's in front of you," one of my classmates said. "We have four rocks in this river. There's one about two feet in front of you, and another one in front of that and slightly to the left. Three feet in front of that there's another one, and to the right of that is another stone. We're going to help you navigate that. Step out with your right foot and you'll feel the first rock. *Boom*. Alright, cool. Now with your left foot, step to your left—there's that stone that's right there in front of you: step right there."

Another classmate was behind me, holding on to my hand to make sure I was good. Another person was on the opposite side, making sure I kept my balance. I shifted my body so I could twist and reach my hand out to them on my other side. They helped me step onto the next two rocks.

"Alright, Lex, you've got the third rock that's in front of you right now: step on that. *Boom*. The last one is slightly to your right: step on that. *Bam*. There's the land in front of you, you're good!"

Stepping onto the shore, I was exhilarated. I felt fearless. It wasn't just that I'd succeeded in crossing the stream; accomplishment alone wasn't enough. I wanted to share that experience with my classmates. Not being able to see the stream was intimidating, but getting across with their support was an exciting experience that has stayed with me. I didn't want to just slingshot across the river; I wanted to experience it like the rest of my classmates.

Sharing this adventure helped us become better at collaborating, trusting each other, communicating, and being vulnerable.

After graduation, I felt like I had a little more leeway to go after some of the things I really wanted to do. In 2008, I was invited to train at the Olympic Training Center, so I moved to San Diego and began focusing purely on athletics as a full-time job. I continued training for the long jump, and I also added the triple jump and 100-meter sprint. I didn't want to just be there to participate, I wanted to make an impact and see what I could achieve—winning golds, breaking records, and creating a legacy.

At the Olympic Training Center, I met professional coaches, and Olympic and Paralympic athletes, and some of them were pioneers of their respective sports. I was able to learn from their experience, albeit begrudgingly.

Growing up, I saw athletes featured on commercials, print ads, and billboards promoting everything from cars and insurance to footwear and drinks. I imagined that they were successful. They probably didn't have to worry about money and most likely paying their bills would never be an issue—they were on TV after all! Once I actually started living in that world, however, I recognized that only a few athletes can just live off the sport. On the Olympic and Paralympic side, building your brand allows you to increase your monetary success, your profile, and your overall value.

The athletes who were doing well—the ones who had pairs of shoes and cases of sports drinks delivered to their doorstep—were active in brand activation. They had sponsorships and speaking engagements. I wanted that for myself. I didn't see—pun intended—many blind and visually impaired athletes getting that type of recognition and being rewarded in that fashion. I thought, *Man, I want to know what that's like. I can do that, too.*

I thought I was in the perfect place: I had access to the people who were doing exactly what I wanted to be doing, so *surely* they would want to share their wisdom and expertise with an up-and-coming athlete.

Think again.

In my initial quest to acquire all those things I wanted to have and do, I got so much resistance from other Paralympic athletes. They told me things like, "You're not good enough yet," or, "You're going to have to break a world record before you get any of those things."

I was pretty new in the sport, and I wasn't anywhere close to a world record.

When I asked them to share their insight into how they were able to get to where they were, the other athletes were not forthcoming. It was as if these amazing athletes thought that by giving me that information, I would potentially be taking food off their plate or money from their pockets. I think their mindset was that there are very few deals available for Paralympic athletes so they needed to safeguard these rare opportunities. We were suddenly in competition on *and off* the track.

I thought to myself, *Alright, if you're not going to share with me, I'll just have to figure it out myself then.*

Society tells me no a lot of the time, so I have been programmed to believe that "no" means "not yet." If these people wanted to be stingy and insecure about their own positions as athletes and entrepreneurs, that was fine. It was just a few people saying no, and it became a challenge for me: I bet I can find *somebody* in the billions of people on this earth who can help me get to where I need to go. This is just a dead-end, so I'll hit a U-turn and find a different road I can take to get to my destination.

Naysayers have a gravitational pull. It's exhausting to be around people who impede your progress. It's important to identify who those people are, because your vision is special —it's something that can transform the world—and I would hate for someone who doesn't have the visual acuity you have to cause you to lose focus or be dragged down. Keep those people at arm's length.

But when you adopt this higher level of thinking, you defy gravity and fly above the challenges and obstacles that try to hold you down. And when you connect with people who see your vision, who are willing to offer their abilities, skills, time, and energy to your vision, you begin to levitate.

You elevate to a higher space in life. That's when you truly learn what it feels like to fly.

Build relationships with people who can help you spark your imagination into reality.

Looking for an Agent

I knew that one of the things those people who were not very forthcoming with information had in common was that they all worked with agents, so I said, "Okay, I need to find an agent."

I didn't know any agents, and I had no idea how to find one, so instead I *became* one.

I created a new email address using my middle name and a made-up last name, and I became my own PR agent. I emailed different organizations and associations to tell them all about this phenomenal athlete from the Raleigh-Durham area of North Carolina. "He's totally blind, so it's pretty fantastic what this kid is able to do!"

I didn't get a lot of traction, but I knew all I needed was one yes to be able to get in the door and do a great job. And eventually it came. From that fake email address, I got my first paid speaking engagement: the Raleigh Sports Council paid me an honorarium to come tell my story.

I was on my way!

But I still didn't know the next step. My time was being consumed with sending emails and trying to coordinate deals, but I didn't really know the lingo, what to ask for or how to ask for it. I needed to find a *real* agent.

I Googled and found an agent list on USA Track and Field's website with a few hundred names—and that's when I realized that I didn't even know what type of agent I was looking for. I learned that you can have an agent who specializes in getting you in certain premier events that have prize money and pay an appearance fee for the athletes to show up. But I didn't need an agent for competition, most of whom dealt with Olympians and Olympic hopefuls; my results at the time didn't resemble what those agents would typically work with to get into a competition, and I hadn't built my name up to the point where I could slide in there just off notoriety.

Eventually, I figured out that I wanted a brand manager or an agent who deals specifically with corporate contracts and sponsorships, so I started emailing all the names on that agent list. Again, I received a ton of nos. A few replied to ask for my results, but after I responded with the answer...crickets. I never heard back from them.

After emailing dozens of agents, I finally heard from two people, Kenneth and Eric, who had a sports agency in Atlanta, Georgia. They took a shot on me and pitched me to a few companies.

My name was starting to get around, we had a good relationship, and Kenneth and Eric took a chance on me when no one else was helping me out. They showed me something similar to what I'd seen with my mom, Coach Whitmer, and a few other people: they saw my potential, and they invested their time in me. People can give money and physical resources, but a time investment is even more meaningful because that's a resource you can't get back.

I didn't end up acquiring any deals at that time, but working with them was a great experience. Kenneth and Eric gave me the insight and knowledge I needed to continue my quest to land the opportunities I desired.

I wasn't going to give up. First, I asked for help and I didn't receive it. Then, I kept asking, and I finally got help ... but what I wanted still didn't happen. I would just have to keep on asking and continue having faith that I could achieve what I wanted.

I listen to a speaker named Myles Monroe who talks a lot about vision, and he once said something along the lines of, "If what you see now is not what you saw then, where you are is not where you're going to be." I took his statement to mean: if you set a vision for yourself in the future, and that's not who you are yet, then you're not done with your journey to get there.

That dropped a bombshell on me, and led to a shift in my vision, refining my purpose from when I was a budding athlete in high school to seeing something bigger for me as a professional athlete and speaker. Instead of thinking I could jump straight from step one to step ten, I was able to stand back and see all the steps I needed to follow so I could continue moving forward.

Right then, I couldn't really say what I needed from a sponsor or why I wanted to become a speaker. If someone asked me, "Why do you want to speak? Who's your audience? Who do you want to speak to?" I couldn't answer; I hadn't started connecting with people yet. I needed more pieces to assemble these things I wanted to be a part of.

I recognized that it wasn't happening for me right then because I was not yet where I needed to be. Status quo wasn't where I was supposed to be; I needed to keep excelling to the next level, and the level after that, and the level beyond *that*. And to make that happen, I needed to keep pushing, to keep calling, and to connect with other people who could help me.

Expand Your Vision

In 2009 or 2010, I was talking on the phone with Coach Whitmer when he brought up an idea he'd mentioned before: "Lex, why don't you reach out to some college students and have them help you build your brand? You need someone to help you—you're getting better in the sport, and this is what

Olympic athletes do. They get sponsors, and that's what helps them purchase equipment, flights, registration fees for competitions, and massages for recovery—and what helps them pay for day-to-day expenses. You can do this, too."

He suggested working with college students because agents were telling me no, but college students with aspirations of working as sports agents or for major sports marketing firms might be more amenable—and they could potentially use our work together for course credit. I'd never pulled the trigger on this before because I wasn't in the right position, but this time I finally thought, *I'm ready for this. I can see this for myself.*

I did some research online and found out that San Diego State University had a Sports Management MBA program. Students in an MBA program already had one degree and were working toward another in a profession they wanted to go into, so they'd probably take the project seriously. That was the sign I needed.

But, once again, it wasn't quite the right time.

In the fall of 2010, I sent an email to the general inquiry mailbox on the sports MBA website, asking if any students were interested in helping me with some brand activation. I didn't hear back, but I was used to radio silence from all those agents who never responded.

Then I had the World Championships in New Zealand in January 2011, and I did well, adding two more medals to my collection. Just five months later, I broke the world record in the long jump.

Then in May of that year, the idea came back to me and I reached out again. Even though one of my biggest fears is to cold call somebody, because it's just so uncomfortable to pick up the phone and make a call out of the blue, I did. My hope was to get their voicemail so I could leave a message instead of having to talk live with another human on the line. I dialed the number of a professor at the university, and he actually picked up. I told him about what I was looking for, and he agreed to send an email out to the department asking if any of the students were interested.

Soon, a student named Kelley reached out to me, teaming up with two other students named Kate and Jenn. They came to the Olympic Training Center in May 2011 so we could sit down and talk about what I wanted to do: branding, sponsorships, and speaking engagements. They could use a lot of the things we worked on as class credit and points on their resumes, so it worked out for all of us.

The three of them were well versed in so many areas, but we decided to assign roles to each student. Kelley became the PR person, Kate was the numbers guru who focused on social media analytics, and Jenn was the social media whiz who helped me with content and knowing what would be interesting for followers and fans. Together, we created a machine: building a website, getting business cards, setting up a Google Voice line, creating brochures, and starting all my social media accounts. They helped me grow my business acumen and shift my mind to see how things worked in the professional space, and I completely trusted them to craft my public persona.

Kate made the connection for my first sponsorship through her involvement at an event at the training center. I was invited to do long jumps at the event, and Kate was there working her magic. From the contacts she acquired at the event, she was able to land a sponsorship deal for a luxury car company.

From then on, whatever I was doing, Kelley, Kate, and Jenn were right there, helping me get from point A to point B, giving me the rundown on how long the event was, telling me what I needed to do, and sharing exciting or interesting things people would want to know about when I did speaking engagements.

They got me started on the right foot and helped me build my brand. Even after they graduated, they stayed involved and even added another person to our team, Elissa, who took the baton from the girls and helped to stretch my reach even farther. Eventually, we needed someone to take on the more complex opportunities that were beginning to roll in, and one of them introduced me to the agent I still have today.

From them, I learned that leaders need to trust their teams fully—and they may be surprised by what their teams can create that they wouldn't have been able to envision alone. These ladies are each amazing themselves, but when we joined forces they connected me to so many people that helped me grow my reach to places I only dreamed of. There were five of us sitting at a table, each of us with different ideas and skillsets, putting them together to bring that vision into reality. I had to lean on each of them because they knew and could see things I had no experience with.

And they helped my vision become a full-fledged reality.

Vision is composed of individuals who have a similar visual acuity, or who see on a similar wavelength. For those moments where I might not have been able to see clearly, Josh and Coach Whitmer and my mom and Kelley and Kate and Jenn and Elissa all helped me cleanse the lens I was looking through so I could expand my gaze. Then they helped bring that vision into fruition.

Sometimes, as a leader, your vision has to become somebody else's vision.

You have to take the time to understand the task, the end goal, *and* each person in the group. Ask questions and get their perspective—what does this mean to you? What does it feel like?—to absorb their vision or mentality. Once you're able to see things how they see them, you're able to understand, to make suggestions and changes, to acquire the same line of sight.

One type of leader just says, "Alright, this is what we have to do. This is what I see, so just follow my lead and do what I say." The people on that leader's team are only looking through one lens, even if that's not the best or most experienced. At the end of the day, a leader is only human; they can't achieve the vision alone.

A different kind of leader, however, takes the opportunity to look through someone else's lens, to see that person's vision, and that expands how the leader sees—and it also expands potential opportunities and possibilities.

Which kind of leader do you want to be?

Leaders get better responses and productivity from their team when the team understands that they believe in them enough for them to contribute to this ultimate vision, that they are all working together to do what's best for that vision as a whole. Embrace these moments to learn and grow. You have people who listen and look to you, and that new knowledge may be crucial to your success *and* theirs.

Seeing Myself as a Speaker

In 2010 I joined the Paralympic Ambassador Program, which selected a number of athletes to go into the community and be a voice for the Paralympic movement. As part of this program, they gave us classes where we learned from presenters and great orators. They taught us how to create an elevator pitch and how to write a longer, twenty-to-thirty-minute speech. They even helped us enhance our improvisation skills. Most importantly, they helped us get comfortable speaking in front of others.

The better speaker I could become, the more opportunities I felt would open up to me for sponsorships. At the same time, as I stood up to speak in front of more people, I became more aware of my own insecurities.

I wanted to become a better speaker but also a better *communicator*—someone who could be a lot more comfortable having conversations and communicating with others, despite my blindness. At the time, I still had some insecurities to work on; I was nervous telling my story in great depth, specifically when it came to my blindness. This new training helped me break through some of those insecurities and relieve that initial anxiety from meeting new people. It also taught me to help ease the minds and nerves of the people I met who may have been meeting a blind person for the first time—and who were probably just as scared as I was.

I knew that all these things would help me get where I needed to go.

I got my first sponsor deal in 2012; by 2014, the sponsorships were coming in waves—and a lot of those sponsorship agreements included appearances to speak at employee engagement events or conferences. I started to see the impact that I was having—and that I could help change minds and perceptions, and make a living doing this.

At the end of the day, when I'm on stage serving as an ambassador for an organization or a brand, it's not about me. Early on, I wondered whether people looked at me a certain way, or whether they thought my eyes looked weird. But all that went out the window when I realized the impact I could have with my story.

I told myself, "If I can get on stage and impact the life of at least one person in the audience, I've done my job." If I could introduce the Paralympics to just one more person, or help the parent of a child with a disability and give them hope and advice, then I'd fulfill my purpose on or off stage.

In 2015, I mentioned to Kate, in casual conversation, "Hey, do you know anybody who can help me get more speaking engagements? I think that's a great way to evolve my brand."

She said, "Have you told anybody that you want to be a speaker?"

"Uh... no," I had to admit.

"Well," she said, "how is anybody going to know that's what you want if you don't tell them?"

Within two weeks, she had connected me with a gentleman in the community who knew someone who was responsible for securing speakers for TEDx San Diego.

Through this connection, the TEDx team invited me to sit down and talk about whether I would be a good fit for their event. Being in the room felt like a job interview. "The theme is 'The Age of Magic,'" one of the team members said. "What kind of speech would you be able to come up with along that theme?"

This was my chance. I took a deep breath and gave him a synopsis of my childhood. I told him that I lost my sight, that I had a number of individuals in my life who got me to change my mindset, and that through those individuals' assistance I was led to athletics.

I told the team how I compete: "I have my guide who stands at the take-off board. He claps and yells so I know which direction to run. He makes sure I'm safe, and his presence gives me the confidence to maneuver down the runway. I count my strides. After my last step, I take off and soar through the air and land in the sand. Every single time I step on that runway, it's a magical experience. That is the one place where no one else can tell me who I am; I know when I step on that runway that I am gifted, that I have the physical talent to run fast and jump far—even though society believes the opposite. When you have a strong vision and you set your path and go after it, you begin to see your dream unravel before your face, and that's a magical experience."

When I finished, there was a pause as the team took the story in.

"That's extremely powerful," one person said. "I think this would be a huge asset to our show. I'll need to circle back with the committee and see how this might fit in our current lineup of speakers. We'll reach out to you as soon as possible."

I felt like I'd killed the meeting, but on the ride home to the Olympic Training Center, I wondered whether they would go for it. As soon as I got home, I checked my email, and there was a message from the team.

"We have one more slot, and it's yours for the taking if you want it."

I fist-pumped the air with excitement and shouted aloud in my dorm room. I immediately hit reply: "I'd love to."

Find Your Collaborators

Who are the people who can help you piece the building blocks of your vision together? Identify who in your life already has the skills you need help with—or write down what those skills are and think through where you can look for people to help you.

The next step is to literally *ask for what you want.* Remember how Kate asked me if I'd told anyone I wanted to be a speaker? Within two weeks she had a connection ready and waiting for me. As my friends say, "Closed mouths don't get fed." So open your mouth and let people know what it is you're trying to achieve, and what skills you've seen in them that can help you down the path. Tell the people who fuel your vision what you want so they can continue to help you.

Finally, get clear on how your vision impacts the world. How does your vision help other people? When you understand that, you'll also understand how your own requests for help turn into help for others.

YOUR VOICE IS A GUIDE

After I told the TEDx San Diego people I'd love to speak...I realized that meant I actually had to do it. Fortunately, I didn't have to do it alone.

People may think that because I can't see, I shouldn't be scared of talking in front of a large crowd...but even if I can't see their faces, it's still intimidating to picture all those people sitting there listening to *me*. I had to nail it.

All the TEDx speakers were given speech coaches to help us design and write our speeches. My speech coach, Fia, and I worked on my messaging during the spring and summer of 2016. Fia helped me dial in what I wanted to say, writing and rewriting until it conveyed exactly my message.

She'd ask me, "What is the point you're trying to get across here? What are you *really* trying to say to the crowd? Let's break it down."

That season I was also tackling another important goal: training for the 2016 summer Paralympics in Rio. In mid-July I took a break from the speech and put my head down to continue preparing for one of the biggest competitions of my career.

Once I was back and recovered from the Rio Paralympic Games, it was crunch time, and I sat down and wrote the speech. I finished it at the end of September 2016, and over the next few weeks, Fia and I met in person to work on my cadence, tone, and delivery. In October, it was go time.

On the day of the event, Fia helped me prepare and guided me where I needed to be. There were twelve speakers, and we were split into three groups of four. I was the last speaker in the first group. When it was time, we went upstairs and stood about ten paces away from the door. I could hear the woman before me, her voice reverberating through San Diego's Symphony Hall. We had done a run-through on the actual stage the day before, and I knew that this place was *big*. I tried not to picture the sea of faces.

Then it was my turn. Fia walked me out on the stage, then turned and walked offstage, leaving me standing alone on a red, circle-shaped carpet.

I talked about where our wings can take us, when we have the diligence, bravery, and courage to find those wings. I wanted everyone to realize how far they can fly, so I shared my story of how I went from seeing the world, to not being able to see anything. How that was so difficult, but I learned the skills necessary to overcome it, and gained complete confidence in my abilities. I wanted everyone in that audience to look within themselves and take the next step to realize their own unique vision of success.

I even sang "Blackbird" by the Beatles at the end of my speech. The moment I finished the last note, I heard the crowd erupt with applause—nearly two thousand people clapping for *me*.

I felt Fia come up beside me, and she just stood there onstage with me for a moment, allowing us both to embrace the applause. Then she said, "You rocked it!"

Her voice bubbled over with excitement and jubilation. After working together on this speech for the past six months, it was awesome to hear her pride at seeing the final product.

Fia walked me off the stage and down the stairs. Because I was the last speaker before the intermission, people were leaving their seats at the same time. They came up to me and said, "I can't contain myself, that was great!"

Someone told me later that I was the only person to get a standing ovation.

Afterward, we migrated to a meet-and-greet room where the audience could say hello and introduce themselves. Kate and her husband, Kevin, Jenn, Elissa, and Wesley were all there. I remembered my conversation with Kate, nearly a year prior, where she asked me, "Why don't you tell somebody that you want to be a speaker?"

And now, with this single event, my life as a speaker changed. It helped me evolve my brand as an athlete, and I started getting more requests to speak. More importantly, that was the day I realized that I have a voice—and that I could use that voice to pierce people's minds, hearts, and souls.

Find Your Voice and Take Flight

After that speech, I thought back to the fellow athletes who refused to share their own career development to help me along, who were protective of their own means of getting sponsorships and deals. At the time I felt these athletes had impeded my progress, but I now realized that my mindset had shifted to, "How can I figure this out? Who are the people who will be transparent and help me out?" I wasn't going to be deterred.

But you don't have to do everything on your own. Have the courage to keep pushing forward, without being silenced. Ask people for help—and if they aren't able to help you, ask if they know somebody who can. You never know unless you ask, and having that help can reduce the amount of time you spend searching for the solution.

Open your mouth and, as parents say to their kids, use your words. You have to tell people what you need, because otherwise they will make their own assumptions, which are likely inaccurate. Somewhere along the way, it becomes easy to forget that we have to ask for the things we want.

But in order to ask for help, we first have to know what we want. We have to uncover our deepest desires. What ideas are magnetic for you? You might not even fully recognize them at the time, but your mind will evoke what's important. My mind continued going back to one idea: *I want to be a successful athlete, business person, and speaker.*

Because that idea reverberated so loudly in my mind, I grew to recognize it as the vision of what I wanted to experience.

What rings loudly in your mind and in your heart? What do you yearn for? These desires make up your internal voice.

Once you can see those desires in your mind, and feel them within you, in order to bring them to fruition, you have to ensure your internal voice is heard—by using your physical voice to express to others what you want to do. Tell them, "I want to make an impact—can you help me? Do you know anyone else who can help me?"

You might be afraid to ask for help because you don't want to hear people say no. Or you might be afraid your dreams will sound silly when spoken out loud to someone else. Or maybe you want the sense of pride that comes from accomplishing things on your own, so your ego tells you not to ask for help. Fear and pride are vision killers when it comes to living out the dream you have within yourself. If no one knows what you want, they can't help you. And if you need help but try to do everything yourself, your end goal gets bottled up inside you. You want it so badly but you *just can't quite get there*, which leads to frustration, anxiety, anger, and sadness—none of which ultimately feed your vision.

Using your voice helps you build a bridge and close the gap between where you are and what your vision shows you is possible. And your voice is not just how you speak, but also that internal voice, the one that guides you.

Whose voice guides you? Who is the person you understand best, both what they say and what they mean?

When babies are first born, they can't see well, but they know their parents' voices, and that's how they know who to turn to. As we get older, that voice becomes drowned out by so many external factors, but I don't want you to lose the ability to recognize the voice that comforts you, that pushes you, that you trust to guide, inspire, and motivate you.

Additionally, how can *you* become that voice for someone? How can you use your voice to create trust, to uplift and empower people at times, but also to bring them back to earth with humility and grace when necessary? How can you become that person who helps others use their power appropriately to navigate down their own runway and soar into their dreams?

Initially, your vision is about your personal desires—improving your life, your current state—but ultimately vision is meant to transform minds, culture, society, and the world. With a genuine, *true* vision, you see something more for yourself, but you also understand that your interaction within this space is going to galvanize your work. People will see how you move and operate, and they'll gain inspiration from your actions. They'll think, "I want to do that, too!" and they'll get an internal kickstart to believe they can operate in a similar capacity.

Vision transcends our personal desires, to create a larger, positive impact in the world. Once I saw how my personal goals were resonating with other people, I started to see beyond my personal vision and asked, "How can I turn up the heat here, to have a greater impact and achieve even *more*, for and with more people?"

As I said in my speech, we all have challenges, but we also have the opportunity to find our wings so we can all soar to new heights and experience true flight.

How can you be a guide for someone else, to empower them and give them the ability to fly?

Honing My Voice

After the TEDx speech, I was offered more speaking opportunities, including for a well-known financial institution and a popular pharmaceutical company. I wanted to make sure my speeches were knockout punches, because I recognized how important those opportunities were.

I reached out to find someone to help me improve how I put my story together, so it could be more impactful. I was connected with a new speech coach who listened to my TEDx speech and said, "It's inspirational, but there aren't any action items here. There's nothing to entice people to go out into the world and apply what you're talking about."

Even though I'd had success with that big speech, I needed to get better. So we started from zero, and she asked me new questions: "What feelings did you have at this time? What types of feelings do you think your listeners will have, as human beings?"

We added more texture and color to the story, emphasizing feelings of fear and uncertainty, challenges with trust or being alone—moments the audience could relate to—and how I got through those moments.

Instead of just telling a story, we turned the speech into

something that could educate my listeners on how to envision their highest goal and then how to gain the courage to take a shot in the dark.

Through this process, getting that assistance helped me shift how I tell my story, turning speaking opportunities into conversations that were more relatable and that connected on a deeper level.

As I was gearing up to speak more, I also did my own research, watching how other speakers portrayed their personalities onstage, and how they got past their inhibitions so they could inspire people.

One of the speakers I really admired were Myles Munroe, who I mentioned earlier. He was a quintessential speaker with a very strong voice, who got animated when he spoke, the passion pouring out of him. I even liked the way he said certain words and the power of the pauses he used in his speeches, letting the silence give the audience time to think about what he said.

I also checked out celebrities and other personalities, like Robin Roberts and Jamie Foxx. While I wouldn't categorize Jamie Foxx as a professional speaker, he is a great storyteller, very vivid with his descriptions. I appreciated the words he used and how he said those words; it made me feel as though I could picture exactly what he was talking about.

All the speakers I learned from, even though they had reached the top of the mountain peak in their respective areas and were very accomplished, also found ways to help the audience remember that they are human—even when describing experiences that the average person likely won't have. They pulled out the humanistic element of the story so their listeners could share in the emotions they've dealt with and the challenges they've fought through.

Their speeches made me feel like I knew them, like we'd been good friends for a long time—and they were the kind of friends who encouraged me to continue challenging myself.

Battling Insecurities

All of this research and preparation was necessary, not just to improve at the craft of speaking, but to help me battle the insecurities I'd had since losing my sight, which were exacerbated by standing on a stage and presenting myself for anyone to see.

My kryptonite used to be my eyes.

Growing up, kids would ask me, "Hey, how many fingers am I holding up?" Or they'd say, "You're not looking at me! What are you looking at?"

When I'm recording videos, it's obviously challenging for me to look directly at the camera because I can't see it. People ask me, "Have you considered wearing sunglasses?" as though my blindness is something I need to hide so other people can be comfortable. On social media, people write in, "Is someone going to tell him to look at the camera?" Or, "Wait—is he blind?"

Each one of those comments represented an emotional blow. I'll never be able to make eye contact with someone. I won't be able to glance across the room and see someone smile. I won't be able to watch television. That might resonate differently for someone who was born blind and has never had those experiences, but I was able to see those things at one point and then the day came when I wasn't able to.

Every time someone pointed out how different I was, I couldn't hear my internal voice any longer. All I heard was doubt.

By now I've built up a tougher shell, but even though those comments don't hit as hard, they still pull on those scabs that have formed. Was becoming a speaker going to open me up to more tiny blows to my armor?

When I first started to speak onstage, I worried about what the audience was thinking. *Do they see me differently because I'm blind? Do they think I'm incapable or undeserving?*

I couldn't see the audience's facial expressions, so I didn't know if they were engaged with what I was saying. I couldn't make eye contact or look directly at them—would that weird them out? Or would they understand?

Soon, I learned that I had to educate people on *me*, a person who has a disability, who is blind. They may not know that a lot of people with disabilities feel different because of how society treats us.

Our diagnoses don't disable us as much as society does.

Even though I was onstage sharing my story, helping people learn to overcome in their own lives, I was also an advocate for a population that is often overlooked and isolated; those audiences could learn how to interact and engage with someone who has a disability.

I wasn't just trying to get the audience to see me, I wanted to help them understand people who are like me—a person with a disability who deals with daily pressure from others who may look at me as "lesser" or "incapable." My speaking is an opportunity to not only share my stories, but to share them in a way that provides education for others to gain a greater awareness that people with disabilities are still out here living successful and meaningful lives. Every one of us has something uniquely special to offer the world, especially when we focus on a person's *ability* rather than their disability. They may possess a skill or talent that could be a game changer.

I overcame my own insecurities by recognizing that people will probably always view me differently, but I can use that as a strength to achieve my vision.

You've likely experienced something similar. Taking the stage as a leader means stepping up in a bigger way, to do something right, even though there may be fear or insecurity attached to doing that. You have to have something to hold onto—something that keeps you interested, inspired, and motivated—even though there may be huge obstacles and barriers in front of you.

When something is on the line for yourself, you work hard at the challenge. But when it's for someone else, especially your team, you turn up the heat even more. When Wesley and I are competing, I want to win for myself, but I also want to win for him. If we can shift our minds to understand it's about more than just ourselves, we can tap into more courage to push past our fear.

Recognize that when your vision requires you to get past this hurdle, or another person is depending on you, then you will need to put aside your ego and insecurities. I know you are facing a fear, but the success for yourself *and* for others is on the line. Can you commit to take action, even in the face of that fear?

That's courage at its purest form. When you believe in something so much that you move closer to it, your belief becomes stronger than your insecurity. Your inner voice can become so strong that it penetrates through your fear.

Turn Your Weaknesses into Strengths

I recently heard someone say, "If *your* strengths look like *their* weaknesses, then they probably won't like you." I think the reverse is also true: if your strengths show up as their weaknesses, then it's an opportunity to educate them.

Speaking didn't start out as a strength for me—it was a weakness. To become a great speaker, I had to face my demons around what other people would think of me or what my blindness might mean to them.

Both in competition and out, people sized me up and tried to determine what I was capable of. When they see someone who is six-foot-ten, they probably assume he plays basketball. But when they see a blind person walk in the door, their minds go somewhere else; they would probably not believe he's a Paralympic track-and-field athlete. They almost became paralyzed, and I could sense that weakness in them—but I worried that they also saw weakness in me.

And, as with any weakness, I looked at it as something to improve. I saw a speaking career as an opportunity to become stronger in the areas necessary for me to be in the best position to help and educate others. Many people may shy away from their weaknesses and try to hide them, but I wanted to lean into that challenge and find a way to use my perceived weaknesses to my advantage. I didn't want to just be a bump on a log, as my mom says; I wanted to galvanize people. I wanted to be the kind of person who helps shatter some of these narratives around people with disabilities.

I remembered what it felt like to transition from being able to see to not being able to. I remembered how hard it was to navigate a college that was so spread out. I remembered the awkwardness, uncertainty, and feeling of shame in having to ask for help.

If there was something I could do to help alleviate some of those feelings in the next person to come along, so they didn't have to deal with those specific challenges, then that's what I wanted to do. I wanted to take this situation by the horns so I could do what's necessary not just for me to succeed but for the success of everyone coming up behind me.

Everything is connected. The actions you take now impact others, directly and indirectly. So I often had to remind myself, *It's not about you.*

When I first got on stage, it felt like it was all about me because I was telling *my* story. But what I came to realize is that even when telling my story, it was in greater service of how other people will perceive people like me going forward.

Eventually, I learned to use my story as a conduit to ask questions and present ideas for the people in the audience. I could tell a story and then talk about how it relates to all of us, as human beings. For example, I could get onstage and say, "I've gone to the Paralympic Games and gotten on the podium five times, I'm doing good—I'm going to get the gold!"

Or I could tell a story about making it to the Paralympic Games and winning silver five times, but not yet achieving my goal of winning gold, and tie that into other times we as human beings feel like we've come up short. So many times in life, we feel like we *just* missed out on an opportunity. When that continues to happen, over and over again, we feel discouraged, stressed, and anxious. It becomes easy to fall into darkness and depression.

But we also have the option to change our mindset, to pull the silver lining from those moments. I could think of myself as coming up short—or I could look at myself as being just one more spot away from where I really want to be. I'm almost there. I'll get gold next time.

The beauty of speaking is that you can use any story that supports your point, pulling the lessons from it so that it resonates with people. They may not understand what it feels like to be a professional athlete, but everybody knows what it feels like to come up short, to lose, or to not make it this time.

After one memorable speech, a gentleman came up to me and told me about himself and his life, and how the stories I told resonated with him. He was just starting his own journey of things he wanted to pursue in life, and he didn't think that his current situation would afford him the opportunity to reach those goals, so he had to make some changes. We kept talking, eventually leaving the venue just to sit on a bench outside and have a conversation. Within that conversation, he said, "You're teaching people to see."

That blew my mind. I had just begun to transition from telling my story to trying to make an impact on other people—and this not only let me know I *could* do it, but also reminded me *why* I was doing it. He told me that my words provided that internal fire, the encouragement he needed to jump from the ledge after thinking about it and questioning it too long. Now, instead of sitting and thinking, he was ready to jump into action.

When you look back at your own experiences, think not just about what was happening, but also what you were thinking and feeling. Although we all have different experiences, the emotions we feel and the thoughts that go through our minds are often similar. Look at your situation and pull out moments where you felt afraid, alone, isolated, or like you wanted to give up. You can express those emotions, and use them to connect to your listeners: "Although our stories might be different, I can imagine how you feel."

Expressing yourself in this way can make you feel like you're out on a limb, like you're naked, vulnerable, and exposed—and that's scary. You don't want people to point and stare, ridicule you, or criticize you. When you put your raw emotions and feelings out there, you might worry you're putting yourself in a position where someone can crush you: *What if they see me, the real me, and they don't like that person?*

A lot of us are reluctant to share ourselves because of our fear that someone else can hurt us. Emotional pain is draining and taxing; it weighs down your mind and can even hurt physically. But the only way for people to get to see who you really are is by making that emotional connection—and that means being open and honest, so they see more of the ways you are similar than dissimilar.

When you can tap into shared human emotions, you give your audience an inside look not just into what you felt and thought, but also what actions you took to conquer a challenge. From there, you may be able to offer some advice or suggestions for how to proceed—but only if you've made that connection to their internal voice by focusing on your own emotions and internal experience.

Challenge People to Be Their Best

When I tell people about becoming a long jumper, about having someone to guide me down the runway, I also challenge them to be that guide for someone else—to be that solid voice so they know which direction to navigate. I want you to be the person who empowers someone else. It's healthy and necessary for leaders to give information, but we also need to give people challenges so they can work to implement that information.

At the beginning of the year, my coach and I set training goals: to achieve a certain speed, jump a certain distance, or lift a certain amount of weight that year. When we get to the end of the year, we measure our progress against those goals to see how far we've come.

Leaders need to continue to challenge those around us, so that we can create positive momentum, so people can work to achieve those challenges and measure their progress against those goals.

Challenging others is how you pull the best out of people. You put the ball in their court and give them the opportunity to take action—and sometimes people are just waiting for permission or encouragement to do so because they can't yet see the potential within themselves.

At a time when I was both literally and figuratively blind, Coach Whitmer was my eyes. He saw that potential in me. In those times I was fearful, he reminded me that I was safe, that he was watching over me, so nothing would harm me, so I could train and compete to the best of my ability. He challenged me to take both that literal and figurative jump. I am where I am right now because of the foundation he created with his encouragement.

As a leader, you have to keep that fire lit so your team continues working to bring that vision into reality. But these challenges are not arbitrary; they should be directly related to the goals you want people to achieve. The benchmarks you measure should lead your team to overcoming any potential obstacles or move you all closer to your goal.

There are times when my coach has something on the workout sheet that I don't feel like doing—but I do it anyway, because I know it will bring me one step closer to where I want to be.

One of the workouts I hate to do is our sprint hills workout. We start with exercises on the track, and because I know what's coming, I feel nauseous. Not because this part of the workout hurts, but because I know how I'm going to feel when it's all done. We wrap up on the track and my coach tells us to go to the bathroom or do whatever we need before the hills.

Then we begin our long walk to the top of a nearby hill. It takes six or seven minutes to get to the top of the hill, and I dread every step. Our coach brings a Bluetooth speaker that rolls on wheels and parks it at the top of the hill. We drop our water bottles next to it. And then we walk across a path to the bottom of the hill.

For the next half hour we sprint up the big hill. We run forty meters up the steep incline as fast as possible. Our coach stands at the forty-meter mark and yells out each athlete's time as they pass him. Once the athletes are at the top, they walk straight back down to the bottom. We run the forty-meter sprint three times before we get a rest.

We get a five minute break—a luxury to prepare for what comes next, which is three rounds of sprints to the sixty-meter mark. At the last sixty, I feel the lactic acid boiling in my glutes and hamstrings. That's when I know this is going to hurt later.

After another break, we run up the whole hill, eighty meters, as fast as we possibly can. Crossing the line hurts badly enough, but then we walk all the way back down the hill to line up for the next rep. The walk down never feels like enough rest. Our breaths get shorter and shorter.

We usually only do two repetitions of the 80 meter sprint instead of three, because our coach knows the last eighty meters will be brutal. By the end, the hill looks like a graveyard with all the athletes splayed out on their backs. We drink water, grab our stuff, and trudge back. It takes an immense amount of strength to put one leg in front of the other when my legs feel like Jell-O. Meanwhile our coach is singing songs, rolling the speaker behind him. "You all right? That was good work today!" None of us respond; we don't want to hear his voice. This is a time I wish I had sight, so I could put my hands around his neck.

The thing that keeps me pushing forward is the fact that I know doing this workout is going to help me. To this point, my coach has helped me win the 2013, 2015, 2017, and 2019 World Championships. We got silver at the 2016 and 2020 Paralympic Games. His training plan has been working. So when I look at those results, I say to myself, *This particular workout is painful... but it's helping me go in the right direction.*

The last time we were about to do this workout in the lead-up to Tokyo, someone said to me, "Lex, you ready to die?"

I tried to find some glimmer of hope at the end of the tunnel, anything to hang onto, and replied, "Well, someone once told me you gotta die first to get to heaven!"

Sometimes we have to just suck it up and make it happen, because where we want to go is more important than where we are right now. You achieve your vision by moving closer to it, closing that gap inch by inch and foot by foot.

Listen to Your Voice

Your internal voice is a guide. What is your internal voice saying to you? What types of things are burning deeply inside of you? What do you hear your guide telling you to do when you're alone and you have time to think and listen? Those things you want, that you have built up within you—your ideas, thoughts, desires—are your starting point.

As you pursue them, your guide morphs: your ideas have to spill out into your physical voice.

Don't just expect things to happen; you have to put rubber on the road. Use your words, talk to other people, and put your vision in motion. Ask for help, ask questions, tell people what you want. Have the courage to dig down deep and expose exactly what you want without any type of reluctance or fear around what another person might say or think. Have the courage to put your desires out there.

Once you put yourself out there, things will begin to happen for you; your vision will become more of a reality. Then you will recognize that while your voice was once just something that lived within you, when you share it with someone else, and they help you get to where you want to go, it can become a guide for someone else.

Become a better listener. Relatively speaking, we can all hear, but not everyone *listens*. When you listen, you're able to comprehend and engage with what someone is saying. Then you can begin to understand: How can I help? How can I do what was done for me, to help their voice and their vision grow?

In this chapter we talked about how achieving your own vision contributes to another person's vision. Similarly, listening to another person helps us understand how we can positively impact them. What guidance can you give? How can you help them reach their dreams?

9 MOVE MOUNTAINS BY LEARNING TO FEEL

In 2016, through one of my sponsors, I was offered the opportunity to throw the first pitch at a Charlotte Knights game, a AAA team in North Carolina.

I couldn't help but think that people wouldn't expect me to excel at this, that they would assume I couldn't throw a strike. I wouldn't be pitching to a batter—I'd throw to the catcher—but I still wanted to hit the strike zone.

When I told my friends I'd get to do this, they joked around and said, "Oh man, don't throw it at a cameraman like Snoop Dogg did!"

Even though it was just for fun, I was nervous. I had to go out there and show these people what's up. I knew if I didn't—if I threw a wild pitch or missed—people would just dismiss me. I could just hear them: "Oh, well, yeah. Of *course* he can't pitch. He's blind!"

I never want people to excuse my efforts because of my blindness. In fact, I have the opposite mentality: I try to do *so* well that it confuses people as to just how much I can actually see.

To confirm, I basically see nothing. When I'm standing outside, I can barely see the light of day—and that's *it*, even in the brightest sun. I wanted people to almost feel deceived when they see what I can do, so they think, "What the heck is going on here? Is he *really* blind? How in the world did he do that?!"

So, to do well and prove to everyone (including myself) that I could do this, I'd have to practice my pitching.

One of my buddies, Kelly, agreed to practice with me. Outside the sports medicine facility at the Chula Vista Elite Athlete Training Center (formerly the Olympic Training Center) is a large stretch of grass. The lawn was big enough for us to practice without worrying about a wild pitch breaking out windows on the building nearby.

Kelly and I measured out the typical distance between a pitcher's mound and home plate. Kelly stood at one end of the lawn and I stood at the opposite end. I set my cell phone on the ground near me, music spilling out of the speakers, so I knew exactly where to stand to be the right distance from Kelly's mitt.

From across the field, I heard Kelly hit her mitt a few times. "Right here, Lex, right here!" she yelled. I locked into the sound of her voice and launched the ball.

I didn't immediately make it. Sometimes I tossed the ball over her head, or too far outside the plate, and she'd have to run to grab it. Sometimes I threw too short, and the ball bounced in front of her. After a while, I began to hear the satisfying *smack* of the ball hitting the pocket of her glove.

I threw that ball at Kelly's glove, over and over again, until my muscles memorized the feeling of pitching down home plate. I listened for the *thwap* of the ball smacking into the glove.

That sound became a magnet for me, like I heard the ball hitting its target *before* I even launched it. Over and over again, I listened to that sound, and each time the ball hit the glove, I thought, *I did it.*

Now I'd just have to do that again, in the game, with everyone watching.

Take Me Out to the Ballgame

I arrived at the stadium in a shirt with my slogan, *No Need for Sight When You Have a Vision.* A lady who worked for my sponsor, Brittany, guided me onto the field. As we walked, I could smell the freshly cut grass. The announcer introduced me to the crowd, and my name and accolades boomed out through the stadium.

He told the audience I was blind, and I would be competing at the upcoming Paralympic trials being held in Charlotte at Johnson C. Smith University. This first pitch was, in a way, being used as a chance to inform the crowd about this major competition being held locally, and we hoped they would come out and support all the athletes who would be competing for a spot to represent Team USA. The hype worked. People began to clap and cheer.

The ground under my feet changed from shorty, springy grass to packed dirt, and I was guided up the incline of the pitcher's mound. The pressure cranked up to a thousand, and my stomach fluttered with nervous butterflies. I just wanted to get *moving*.

This was my one and only opportunity to replicate that sound I loved so much, now on a professional ballfield. I wouldn't get a do-over; I had to throw this ball right down the pipe.

Finally, the announcer said, "Ladies and gentlemen, give a Charlotte Knights welcome to Lex Gillette!"

The catcher was crouched down behind home plate. I could hear him hitting his mitt with his fist, so I knew right where he was. I took a moment to listen, just standing there on the mound with the ball in my hand, feeling the stitching under my fingers as I turned it. The catcher spoke: "Come on, Lex. I'm right here."

A switch flipped in my brain. *It's showtime.*

I cocked my arm back, zoned in a final time on where the catcher was waiting with his mitt extended, confident that the ball would follow through and smack that glove. Then I unwound and let it go with all my strength behind it.

Thwack.

As soon as the ball left my hand, I just *knew* I got it in the strike zone. I thought, *Right on the money.*

The ball found its target, and the moment the ball resounded against the leather of the catcher's mitt, the crowd went bananas. After the pitch, I was guided down to home plate to take photos. The catcher leaned in and said, "Man, you really got some sting on that!"

Phenomenal, 100 percent intrinsic satisfaction. I had done exactly what I set out to do.

From the Kitchen to the Ballpark —and Beyond

That moment was the culmination of all those times I had thrown the ball to myself in the kitchen when I was a kid, imagining being a ballplayer in a stadium and narrating my highlights. That kid could only dream about hearing his name over the loudspeaker in a stadium, and think, *I want that.*

I still knew that I wouldn't be able to turn a double play, score the winning run, or jump up against the wall to snatch a home run away from someone. But I liked knowing that, by tapping into the skills I'd developed in childhood, I was able to live out a scene that once existed only in my imagination.

It's important to find those spaces where you can just be you, unconfined by any boundaries. For me, that place is the world of sports. In that world, I feel free. Sports don't judge me.

Find those spaces where you can be vulnerable without having to worry about fitting into any preset parameters. You don't have to follow trends or move in step with the masses, traveling in the same direction as everyone else, just because that's what they expect you to do.

The direction of the masses may not align to the feeling you're trying to experience, like the people who were astonished that my mother would allow me to try to do a cartwheel. I wasn't going to stop because they were uncomfortable; to do so would go against the feeling I was trying to experience: not only the physical sensation of my body moving from right side-up to upside down, but also the feeling of my mom being proud of me and my friends being impressed and accepting of me.

Sometimes we feel like we *have* to go in the same direction as everyone else, instead of having the courage to carve our own paths. Trust that the feeling you want to chase is valid, even if it doesn't seem to lead directly to your desired results in the moment. I had to trust that throwing that ball against the kitchen wall was going to lead me *somewhere,* even if it wasn't going to ever get me into a professional baseball career.

I made my dream a reality by focusing on what I wanted to feel—then I took that same skillset and applied it to track and field and becoming a speaker. Just as I came to understand how changing the angle of my arm affected where I threw the ball, I had to learn when to raise my voice and when to say something softer, when to ask for audience participation and when to wait for the crowd's response.

It all comes back to that feeling. When I'm standing on stage, I *know* when things are going in the right direction. I can crack a joke and hear the crowd laugh, right on cue. I might hear a sniffle as a result of telling a poignant story. Hearing someone gasp or murmur mm-hmm," reminds me of being in church, listening to the congregation do a call-and-response with the preacher. Those auditory responses from my audience might as well be an "Amen!"

And when I come off the stage and have the opportunity to chat with people, they often confirm that we were all sharing the same feelings in those moments.

Sometimes we forget to feel. Or we're so driven by what our eyes see, and how that dictates we "should" feel. Our core feelings are out of sight, out of mind when we're at work, looking at a computer screen. We're just focused on getting our coffee, or our lunch, counting down the hours until 5 o'clock.

But life, for me, is literally dark. I don't see anything. If I focus only on what I can see, there's not much to be excited about. I don't see anyone around, so I'm alone. I feel isolated and disconnected. Instead, I choose to focus on what I want to feel, and I refuse to be bound by what my eyes see or don't see. My gaze tells me "there's nothing here," but my vision has allowed me to see beyond that. I don't want to feel lonely and dark; I want to feel the satisfaction of catching the ball in my mitt and the smile it brings to my face. I want to feel the shiver of excitement when I hear a crowd cheering after the swoosh of a basketball net tells me the ball soared through it. Those things make me happy and take me back to my childhood.

I reconnect to those childhood feelings in my adult life, too. I'm always evaluating, "What's the equivalent of that in my career or with my personal goals?"

I take those feelings with me everywhere; I latch on to that feeling of achievement and accomplishment and use it as a measuring stick for every environment I step into. If it doesn't measure up to that feeling, I might need to leave—or maybe I need to work a little harder. I might need to think about the situation differently so I can feel that ball smack into my mitt and hear the ball go through the hoop.

People get sucked into the daily drudgery of what's in front of them; I focus on how I can keep creating the feelings I want to feel. How can I create World Series-esque moments? How can I hear the crowd in my mind go wild? That's what drives me.

How Do You *Feel*?

When I was throwing and catching that ball in the kitchen, I was confident. I had the attitude that I would never give up—even when I didn't catch the ball. Sometimes it would zoom right by me, and I'd have to lie on my stomach and sweep my arms out to either side, trying to find where the ball had rolled on the floor. But I didn't allow those moments to derail my progress.

I brought that same energy to trying to hit the perfect cartwheel, handstand, and flip. I applied it to building my relationship with sponsors and learning which direction to go. When it was a head-on opportunity, I made sure I was in the best position to flip my glove up, catch it, and secure the play.

The most important thing I learned was how to *feel*.

When I first lost my sight, I held my head down in that woe is me way. I (understandably) had a difficult time processing that I *had* been able to see... but now I never would again. So, at first, my mom provided that confidence and motivation for me. I leveraged her strength and ability to persevere.

Once I was able to feel those within myself, I went through a literal transformation in my self-image. My mom, and those other amazing individuals in my life, helped me change the vision I had of myself.

The way you see yourself triggers how you step forward in life. If you see yourself as a great player for this team, or a great candidate for this job, then you will probably be that great player or candidate; you know you have the appropriate skills, the adequate knowledge, and the demeanor or confidence to boldly step into those situations.

The people who make wildly amazing things happen in life have developed that skill. They have taught themselves how to feel, and they know exactly what they want to feel.

Because of that, they become juggernauts. Whatever they participate in, their journey in life has helped them to have high confidence and the ability to persevere, so their intentionality is untouchable. They don't ask, "Where's the barrier?"; they bust through walls and move mountains to make things happen.

Your Best Moments Are Your Internal Barometer

What are the things that bring a smile to your face? What are your favorite moments in life, and how can you use those as a barometer in your quest to succeed? Don't forget about those feelings. Find a way to transcend beyond your sight and bring those feelings to whatever environment you occupy.

What feelings or memories tug on you? Think back to those moments, and tackle your reality with the goal of tapping into the most heartwarming, loving, energizing feelings you can bring with you every day. Anchor into those past memories to build your future vision of what you want to feel. You might not make it to the World Series either, but there's no reason you can't hear the crowd cheering for you!

10

YOUR COURAGE IS JUST BEYOND YOUR FEAR

My buddy Brandon served overseas in the Marines where he was shot, injuring one of his arms. He ended up finding Paralympic sports and decided to train for the upcoming 2012 Paralympic Games in London, which is how we ended up as roommates.

For months, Brandon had been asking me to go skydiving with him. There is a facility called Skydive San Diego near us and he wanted to check it out. I always replied, "Uh, that's okay. I'm good."

But he was persistent: "Come on, man, we gotta go."

"Nah, can't do it."

I knew he'd wait a bit and then just ask me again, so I needed a different response. I was ready the next time he asked.

"Let's go skydiving!"

"I can't," I told him. "Black people don't skydive."

I was throwing out *any* excuse not to do this.

Then, one Saturday morning, Brandon brought it up again: "Let's do it. We gotta go skydiving."

I don't know why—he must have caught me at just the right moment—but I finally gave in. "Alright, let's do it."

"Really?"

"Yeah, man," I said. "Let's go skydiving."

We got in Brandon's F150, stopped at the bank so I could grab the $200 I'd have to pay to put my life on the line, and drove to the skydiving center. On the way, Brandon was so excited, but all I could think was, *Let's hurry up and do this before I change my mind!*

When we got there, they had us watch a safety video and basically sign our lives away. Then we were introduced to a trainer who prepped us on all the rules and explained the body positioning we should have when we jumped out of the plane.

Finally, we met the instructors we'd be strapped to for our tandem jumps. I was introduced to a woman named T who told me she had taken more than fifteen thousand jumps. When she told me that, I thought, *Alright, cool. She probably knows what she's doing.*

Honestly, I was also happy to be jumping with a female instructor, because I felt confident that she would double- and triple-check everything, and I thought she would be more nurturing. That thought comforted me somewhat—not that there's anything wrong with a male instructor.

We walked outside, and I could hear the plane's engines directly in front of where we were standing. It was time.

What You Tell Yourself You Can Do . . . Becomes True

I knew that once I got on that plane, I'd have no choice but to jump out. (Although, thinking about it now, I was probably wrong. I'm sure that if someone got into a situation where they couldn't jump, the pilot would just bring them back down.)

Any time fear crept into my mind, I thought, *You can't think this way. If you do, you'll never get on the plane, let alone jump out of it.*

And that was the goal: to jump out of an aircraft. I didn't know exactly what would work to achieve that goal; I had never done this before. But I knew what *wouldn't* work: telling myself something like, "Oh, there's no way you can do this!"

Instead, I told myself I was going to be one of those many people who are able to successfully get from the airplane door to the ground.

You can't always know what will work to accomplish your goals, but you can determine that something definitely won't work by saying to yourself, "This is not going to happen." If that's your attitude, then it will be 100 percent true. It won't happen—not because you can't do it, but because you decided not to.

The opposite is true, too. When you tell yourself that you *are* going to do something, even if you don't know exactly how at that moment, it becomes possible. You become capable of more than you think.

So ask yourself what you want to see, feel, and touch. What do you want to accomplish? You can do all of those things—but you have to remove those mental barriers and limitations put in place by your fear. Keep digging, keep working, keep pushing forward. Take that risk.

If you do, you just might discover that you can fly.

Locked In

It was time to board the plane. I asked Brandon if I could go first, saying, "Man, I just want to get this over with." I figured if I could board first, I'd be the first person to exit once we were in the sky.

T led me onto the plane first, and everybody else followed behind us. We sat on benches along the sides of the plane, me and Brandon on one side, the instructors on the opposite side, facing us. It must have looked like we were sitting at picnic tables, only without the table part.

The plane began to move down the runway. It accelerated, and the nose lifted off the ground. Then the whole plane rose into the air, and we were off. We flew higher and higher. The door was open the whole time, so everyone could probably see the ground falling away outside.

I was seated near the cockpit, so I couldn't hear much of the environment outside the plane, but I could hear people talking and laughing around me. The facilitators' voices were calm and confident; for them, it was just another day at work. The other participants—especially the first-time jumpers like me and Brandon—had more nervous energy. There were probably eight or nine tandem pairs, like us, and a handful of people who were jumping solo.

Brandon and I chatted a bit, and he cracked a bunch of jokes, but I could only manage a few nervous laughs. I kept thinking in disbelief, *I can't believe I'm on this plane right now!* That feeling consumed me more than the fear. I just never would have thought I'd be on a plane, preparing to jump out the door, strapped to another person, from thirteen thousand feet in the air.

In situations where I'm trying to wrap my head around what's happening, I tend not to talk much; instead, I'm listening and observing what's going on around me. If this had been any other plane ride, I would have put my headphones on and said, "Let me know when we land."

For this flight, however, I was in the moment. I used my powers of observation to cut through the fear and uncertainty. I felt every move the plane made, each little shift as it climbed through the air. In general, the other conversations on the plane were just noise, but when I heard specific words like jump, plane, or parachute, they cut through the chatter and stood out vividly. They were pertinent to what was going on around us, not just mundane conversation, so I listened and tried to sort through the information.

This has become a habit throughout my life. Whenever I experience something new, exciting, or nerve-wracking, or something that creates a little fear—even just being in a new group of people—I use those situations as an opportunity to observe. When I'm quiet, I'm able to tap into all my senses and abilities—what I can smell, hear, taste, touch, what I feel and understand—to take everything in, so I can create an image or path of how to move forward.

For example, when I'm walking around, especially if I'm navigating a new path by myself, I'm not saying much. I'm locked into how the sidewalk feels under my cane and feet, recognizing where there might be a divot or crevice, noticing that with some intersections I can line myself up perfectly in the middle and make a beeline to the other side, to land directly on the opposite curb cut, whereas other intersections might be a little shifted or oblong, so I can't just walk straight ahead when I cross: I need to shift to the right a bit because of how the street is positioned.

When I'm walking, I'm listening to peoples' voices. Are they on my left or my right? That helps me make a decision about how to maneuver. I listen to the flow of traffic. Is there a car on my left side or my right? When I stop, it doesn't really matter to me whether I'm at a stop sign or a stoplight, because I can't see either one. When I reach an intersection and hear the sound of flowing traffic crossing in front of me, it's a good indicator to stay put. An idling car that I hear on my left side is confirmation that it probably isn't safe to cross right now. Once that car begins to roll forward across the intersection, that lets me know it's safe to walk to the opposite side.

But let's say I'm walking down the street in San Diego, where the weather is nice and, especially with the ongoing pandemic, most restaurants have some kind of outdoor dining setup, often on patios that spill over onto the sidewalk or even into the street by the curb. When I approach those areas, it's noisy. I can hear forks and knives clanking against plates, people talking and laughing, even cheering, loud music. In that situation, my mind is already calculating, *How are we going to maneuver through this?*

I may even feel a little uneasy, but I'll calm down by focusing on what I know—for example, that five blocks down and three blocks to the right is a phenomenal pizza place, and pizza is one of my favorite foods. What am I going to do: Stop? Or find a way to navigate from where I am to that pizza place so I can eat and have a good time? I know a couple of those blocks have outdoor seating, and I'll need to weave through the middle of tables like I'm walking down an aisle. One of the streets has trolley tracks on the ground, and the feeling of the rails under my feet is a landmark to me. I know I've got two more blocks to go. Then I can walk a few more steps and take a right turn into the door that leads to my pepperoni pie!

When I need to use my entire being to overcome some kind of challenge or obstacle, I'm not talking on the phone, texting, or trying to hear the TV. I need to use every part of my senses and abilities so I can climb to the top of this figurative mountain. Because once I begin to let in some of those external distractions, I worry whether or not these sounds will divert my attention away from something I need to know, which amplifies the feeling of uncertainty or nervousness. So I need to just lock in, stay focused, and get to where I'm going.

In this case, I was going right out the door.

Time to Jump

As I was locked in on everything happening around me, the plane slowly ascended to five thousand feet, then six thousand. Higher and higher, all the way up to thirteen thousand feet.

T told me she and the other facilitators had watches that gave them lots of information like temperature and altitude. I assumed that's how they were able to determine we'd reached the right height for the jump. I didn't hear a pilot tell them when they were ready; the facilitators just seemed to know. Maybe they had done this so many times, they knew it was almost time based on what the plane did or something they saw outside.

One facilitator said, "Alright, guys, we're good to go now."

T said, "Let's get ready."

I stood up, turned around 180 degrees, and sat basically on T's lap so she could connect our harnesses. That's when I realized: we'd be jumping out of the same door we came in. I'd wanted to be the first person to jump, but by boarding the plane first, I'd guaranteed that I'd be the *last* person out that door. I had to wait until everyone else jumped—and I had to hear every single one of them scream as they left the door for the sky. I felt numb with fear.

The first tandem group jumped out, then, after a brief pause so they weren't jumping right on top of each other, the second group went. As people jumped out, T and I shimmied down the bench, closer to the door. In my mind, I could see the gaping hole of the plane door, the people lined up to jump into thin air, the terrifying drop that awaited them. My anxiety ratcheted up another several notches.

Then it was our turn.

Somehow, I found the strength to move toward the door. I felt T helping me maneuver forward. She extended her arms, holding on to either side of the opening. I heard the engines, much louder now, and felt the rushing wind. T said, "On the count of three, we're going to go."

There's no turning back now.

"One."

You only have one way out of this plane.

"Two."

You have to jump.

"Three!"

And bombs away, we were off. I allowed my body to fall forward as T propelled us from the door. Immediately, we were out there, away from the walls of the plane, just engulfed in sky. I had that feeling in my stomach, like when you get to the top of the hill on a roller coaster and you're just suspended there until finally something unlatches and you go plummeting down the hill but your stomach stays behind, still in the air, for a second or two.

Once my stomach caught up with the rest of me, it was

like being in a convertible with the top down. The wind rushed at my face and I screamed, "This is so wild! Whoooo!"

After a little while, I felt a tug on my body, and we started to slow down. T had pulled the cord to deploy our parachute. We were still traveling down toward the ground, but at a much slower pace. We weren't there yet, but I was confident that we would make a successful landing. I felt it in my entire body. *I'm alive.*

While we were floating, T showed me different tricks based on how she controlled the parachute. We did 360s, spinning in circles like a kid twirling around with their arms spread out. She taught me how to pick up speed by making the parachute smaller and how to slow momentum as well. I guess it took us five or six minutes from when the parachute deployed to when we landed, so we had time to just cruise, chitchatting and laughing the rest of the way down.

Finally, T told me that we were getting close to the ground and that we'd be landing soon. I could also hear voices below, so that let me know how fast the ground was coming up.

She said, "It's not far away now."

We lifted up our legs, keeping them straight out, parallel to the ground, so our bodies and legs formed an L shape. Then T said, "Alright, we're going to touch the ground in three... two... one."

It wasn't the softest landing—in fact, it was a jolt—but it was successful. We made it to the ground. I checked myself over: I was alive, breathing, heart beating. The goal was achieved.

Brandon ran up to me: "How was it, Lex?"

I couldn't even process everything yet, so I gave him one of my typical, downplayed responses. "Man, that wasn't bad at all."

Three Feet Farther

The truth is, skydiving was a lot of fun. It pushed me to do something I'd never done before—and it helped me push past my fear.

There have been many times I have had to face my fears: learning to navigate after losing my sight, going to a new school, starting a new job, learning to long jump, and becoming a speaker. Early in life, I learned that opportunities await you if you're willing to not just face those fears but push past them. When I went skydiving, I discovered just how far I was willing to push myself.

But why is it important to keep pushing? Well, I like to quote something I read in *Think and Grow Rich* by Napoleon Hill: that your courage is three feet farther than your fear.

In the book, Hill tells the story of a man who caught

wind of a gold mine out in Colorado. He trekked out to a promising spot with a pick and shovel and began digging. After a few weeks, he finally struck gold—big gold. So he went all in, borrowing money from relatives and neighbors to bring heavy equipment out to the site to get all the gold they could. But after a bit of drilling, he lost the vein. He kept drilling, searching for where he could pick the vein back up, but eventually concluded he'd never find it. He sold the equipment to a junk man at a loss.

The junk man, meanwhile, asked a mining engineer to take a look. The mining engineer looked at the fault lines of the site and realized the first man had stopped drilling when he was only three feet from more gold. The junk man struck the gold three feet further down, all because he asked for help from an expert.

This story highlights the importance of focusing on the details and taking in sensory information, just like I try to do whenever I'm in a high-pressure situation, as when I was on the plane. I believe your courage lies just beyond your fear. When we feel afraid and want to give up, sometimes we just need to take in more of our environment, and ask for help from someone who knows how to support us. I'd struck a certain level of "gold" in my life, but there was still more possibility there—including winning an actual gold medal. Going skydiving was a way to show myself how to push through my fear so I can create new experiences.

Another time this served me well was when one of my friends who lives in the Bay Area invited me to go sailing with her and her boyfriend on their sailboat in San Francisco Bay. I'm not afraid of sailing in theory, and I know how to swim (although, had anything crazy happened, it would have been a little scary trying to swim through the bay), but it was an unfamiliar experience for me.

When we got on the boat, they showed me how things work as they did what they needed to do to sail the boat. We chatted some, but I couldn't focus much on the conversation. It was really windy, especially on the water, and I was locked in on the feel of the boat as it tilted from left to right. Sometimes it would be tilted so far over, for minutes at a time, that I could reach my hand over the side and touch the water. In my mind, there were a few moments I was certain I'd have to dust off the ol' backstroke.

I used my innate ability to position my body in a way that was comfortable, so that when the boat was tilting, I didn't have to lean in the same direction. By listening to my surroundings and almost becoming one with the boat, I determined the correct way to shift my weight and maintain my balance.

My ability to feel and understand what's going on goes to a different level when I'm in new environments. New situations can be paralyzing with fears, nervousness, and uncertainty, but for me they foster a natural ability to lock in and observe at a high level to make the best decisions. Success often comes after breaking through those barriers, but feeling fear or discomfort can keep you away from something amazing.

When fear takes hold, it's hard to trust that you're only three feet away from finding gold. You worry that you'll be stuck in that uncomfortable place, digging forever. If you can see the benefits on the other side, it's easier to take the leap.

Courage comes into play when you can't see how that benefit can become a reality, so you're left leaping blindly (literally or figuratively) into an abyss.

When Brandon kept asking me to go skydiving, I was curious what it would be like, but I held back on the doorstep of fear: Why would I want to jump out of a plane from thirteen thousand feet up? All the excuses I gave him were just limitations I put on my own mind.

I had those same feelings the first time I did the long jump: You could get hurt, you might run into something, you could twist your ankle. In both cases, my mind was filled with only the negative possibilities of what might happen. I couldn't see the benefits.

But I finally reached that tipping point where my curiosity outweighed my fear. I started to think, *Let's just see what happens.*

Sometimes you have to push those thoughts aside and just go after it, to see what happens. That's what helped me step past that fear. I was not going to allow it to win.

When we're uncomfortable, our first reaction is often not to engage with the fear at all. But in those moments, nothing gets done. We're frozen, engulfed by fear and victim to the feelings of discomfort—and that's what lets those negative emotions win.

Instead, I learned to embrace those uncomfortable moments as growing pains and think, *Let's see what's ahead.*

Those are the moments when we can build up a tolerance to our fear.

I now feel a lot more comfortable with fear, anxiety, and discomfort, because I know I'm always going to feel those emotions, especially during trying times—and I also know that they can help me along this journey.

I can even use that fear I felt about skydiving to help put other moments in perspective. The first time I took an international flight by myself was really scary. But I thought, *I already put my life on the line and jumped out of an airplane.* So many negative things could have happened then, but they didn't. And this was just boarding a plane, flying (and staying inside the plane!), then landing in another country where there would be people waiting who could help me get where I needed to be. How scary could it really be if I didn't have a parachute strapped to my back?

As it turns out, not so scary after all.

That may seem like a small example, but it's those

everyday moments that make us fearful—and those same moments that can help us have courage.

Fear is inevitable. You are going to face situations that cause disruption and discord, that make you uncomfortable. The beauty is in trusting and believing that when you have those feelings, you're on the doorstep of being able to unlock a new magical experience or an amazing achievement. Trust that when you tap into your courage, you'll find the confidence to be bold and move forward in the face of fear. Trust in your ability to push forward and put yourself in the best position to unlock something incredible.

My life as a person who can't see anything has afforded me a lot of opportunities I would have never imagined. Similarly, you might be in situations where you can't see the road ahead—and that puts you and I on the same playing field. You can't physically see how things will play out, but if you can embrace those feelings and have confidence that when things feel uncomfortable and disruptive, you're getting closer, you'll grow that much more and get to new levels. Tap into your ability to feel, observe, and lock in to your vision, so you can ride the wave of courage past what your mind thinks in that moment.

Fears, Real and Imagined

None of this is to say that I *never* felt fear again.

After moving into a new building, I had to go down into the basement to pick up a package in a designated area where all the packages were delivered. The area was fenced in, with a door in the fence that opened with a key fob. From there, we could scan a barcode to open a specific locker and grab the package.

I took the elevator down to the basement, deep underground. The doors opened. I obviously couldn't see anything, but I knew it was dark down there. I thought, *This is the perfect set for a horror film.*

I stepped out into the corridor. Somewhere in all that dark, open space was the door I needed to find, to access the area where my package had been delivered.

But I couldn't find it.

I felt along the walls with both hands, trying to determine where to go. The space was a rectangle, maybe ten feet by fifteen feet, and I walked all the way around it, again and again, trying to find any indication. There was nothing.

I knew it had to be there. I had been here before, with someone helping me, and this was the way they had led me.

I started to get worried, and my brain sensed that fear and ran with it.

Finally, I touched a door handle. It turned in my hand, but I didn't pull the door open. I didn't think it was the right door, and I was worried an alarm would go off. I let go of the door handle. I walked around the perimeter again. Nothing.

I walked back to the door and turned the handle, imagining a ghostly figure haunting me, just waiting for me to open the door and let loose the horrors on the other side. I just *knew* there was a shadowy hand waiting to grab me. If that door had stuck or groaned as it opened, I would have run as fast as my feet could take me.

I told myself, *You have to just do this. Make it happen.*

If there was something on the other side, it was going to get me. I'd just have to deal with that if it happened.

I worked up my courage and pulled the door open. I took a step forward...and I was in a parking garage. I could hear cars driving in and the echo of my shoes on the pavement in the cavernous space. *Oh, that's right,* I thought. *We came through the parking garage to get to the package lockers.*

With my right hand, I felt along the wall until I touched the cool metal fence that served as the boundary to that area. I followed that until I found the door, swiped the fob to get inside, picked up my package, and got out of there.

That fear of something malevolent on the other side of the door was obviously an imaginary fear, but it was strong enough to give me the creeps.

There were real fears there, too. It was so scary to think I knew where I was going and then end up turned around, losing my sense of direction, and worrying I wouldn't be able to get out or go back where I came from. I didn't know the area well, so I could have potentially hurt myself in the unfamiliar environment. I was even afraid of the embarrassment that could have ensued if someone else had come down on the elevator and seen me running around with both hands out, feeling up the walls. What if they had said, "What the heck is this guy doing?"

We all have these imaginary fears or perceived limitations. Looking back now on that situation, did it really matter how I looked, as long as I achieved my goal? Of course not. I was in a vulnerable position, but I would have been able to do what I set out to do, even if I suffered a little embarrassment by someone finding me and asking, "What are you doing? Is everything okay?"

So many people worry about how they look or sound or what other people might think about them. But those worries can kill your self-esteem—and your progress. At the end of the day, it doesn't matter what you look like, if someone thinks you're different or weird, or even if you feel embarrassed. All that matters is that you make it to your desired endpoint.

Find Your Calm

I have a buddy named John Register who served as a mentor to me on my speaker journey, and who is a speaker himself. He talks about resilience, the ability to bounce back and overcome, and shares that within the word "resilience" is the word "silence."

As we talk about moments of discomfort, disruption, nervousness, and fear, how can you find silence? When I was on the plane and heard people chattering, I could tell they were nervous. There are benefits for us in these moments to be silent, listen to ourselves, listen to our bodies, and learn what is going on externally.

How do you fit within this current situation or environment? Tap into what you can feel and what you can observe. Are you aware? How can you use the info you get from your observations to put one foot in front of the other; step past your fear, uncertainty, and nervousness; and step boldly into your courage?

WHEN VISION NEEDS A REVISION

In 2011, I participated in the World Para-Athletic Championships in New Zealand. I qualified for the long jump, the triple jump, and the 100 meter, and somehow I was also entered in the 200 meter race.

There was a bit of a debacle with my long jump, and I didn't qualify for the finals. When I landed, they measured the length of the jump and called out the marks. I'm not quite sure if I was jumping from the correct area, or if the officials measured the marks correctly, but something was terribly wrong. My marks were significantly shorter than normal. Perhaps we made a mistake in measuring my runway approach in the time we had to prepare immediately before the event. Maybe the tape was placed at the wrong spot in relation to the take-off board. I have no clue.

If I'd underperformed, I'd say I just didn't have it that day and take the loss. But something didn't add up. During this particular season, my long jump marks were somewhere in the range of 6.3 to 6.4 meters. Just four months after New Zealand's World Championships, I'd go on to break the world record with a jump of 6.73 meters. But somehow the officials were recording my jumps around 5.0 to 5.1 meters, more than four feet shorter than usual. While some jumps may be outliers, significantly shorter or farther, this was a *huge* difference.

Whatever it was, my best mark didn't secure me a spot in the finals of the event that is my bread and butter.

The long jump is *everything* to me, so after that blow, nothing else seemed important. It felt like someone was driving a knife in my back. I remembered how, when I was a kid, a friend and I would go fishing from time to time and we'd bring home our catch. On one of those occasions, he taught me to scale and gut the fish. That's what I felt like—like somebody had cut out my insides. I had been doing the long jump since high school, at least ten years. This wasn't anything new. I was used to this. This was *my* event. So not making the finals? I was gutted.

Even if I didn't win, I should have *at least* been in the

finals! Once I saw the results, it drove it home even more: I should have won.

But it didn't happen that way.

Gotta Keep Running

To add insult to injury, after that deflating moment with the long jump, I still had to run the 200 meter.

My expectations weren't high. In fact, because this wasn't an event I normally ran, I was certain my competitors weren't expecting me to do much. It was my very last event of that World Championships, my last opportunity to add another medal to the bronze I had already won in the triple jump. All I could think was, *Well, there's nothing to lose.*

Wesley and I walked out onto the track for the prelims, and he helped me get my starting blocks set up. The moment continued to grow, becoming bigger. It was exhilarating right before we were about to run, nervousness combined with excitement. *It's almost time.*

When the announcer said, "On your marks," we placed our feet against the blocks and put our hands on the ground. Wesley was on my right side. I had the tether wrapped around the middle and ring fingers of my right hand. Wesley had a couple of fingers looped on the other side of the tether to lock us in, so we were connected and could run together successfully.

Then they said, "Set," and we got into the starting position, pushing our feet against the blocks and raising our hips, like we were about to pounce.

Then the gun went off, starting the race, and from there it was all a blur. All I knew was that I had to get around this track as fast as possible.

I could hear runners on either side of me. There's a curve in the beginning of the 200-meter track, and Wesley ran on my right side, navigating and helping me curve to the left. He talked the entire way, giving me that auditory feedback: "Keep going! In, in, in. Alright, alight."

Once we were on top of the bend in the track, we began to straighten out. Then it was running straight the rest of the time. Wesley was right there, telling me exactly what I needed to do and where I was in the race, painting that picture for me: "You got fifty meters left. Come on, there you go! We're on the straight; pick it up. Come on, Lex! Twenty meters left! Ten meters. Lean!"

And then we made it across the line. I wasn't sure where I finished within the heat I was in, but once all the heats were complete, the official results were posted on the Jumbotron. Wesley slapped me on the back and said, "We're in the finals, baby!"

I said, "Alright, cool!"

I didn't really know what to expect, but I thought it was great that I'd at least have a shot at medaling. I had made it to the finals of an event I was not accustomed to, but at least I'd run on the track earlier, so I'd gotten to know its unique peculiarities. All tracks are different, but I had an idea of the layout, the curve and the straightaway. I'd be a lot more comfortable in the next round.

That evening, after a few hours of rest in our hotel, Wesley and I boarded the bus to the stadium to warm up for the 200 meter finals.

This was really the last event, and I was ready to let it all out. There was no reason to hold onto any extra energy. I needed to exhaust everything I had in the tank for this race.

We went through the same warm-up and pre-race routine as we normally would, but when we walked out on the track this time, I was a little more confident. I had been able to run and stick with my competitors in the first race, so I should be able to do it this night as well. I felt a heightened level of confidence, and stronger energy and drive.

I felt my spikes gripping the track as we did a couple warm-up runs, and I began to visualize the race, hearing that gun, thinking about getting out of the blocks and running. There were containers behind each set of starting blocks for each athlete to put our belongings in. We removed our warmups—pants, jackets, tops that we wouldn't wear in the competition—and placed everything inside the basket. I did a few bunny hops, up and down, to get the juices flowing.

Wesley leaned in and told me, "You're ready for this. I know things might not have gone the way you wanted in the long jump, but we're here—and you're one of the best athletes in the world. I get to see it every day, and we have one more opportunity to put it on display. Even though being in this event was kind of a surprise, let's go out there and make it happen. I'm going to be right here with you. I got you. We're going to do this, and we're going to do it well!"

His words held a lot of weight for me. I started track and field relatively late in life, as a teenager, but Wesley had been in track since he was a young kid, and he's seen a lot of talented athletes. We'd been working together for so long, so to hear him say that he believed I could make this happen invigorated me and gave me hope. And he was right—I knew I had to go all out, that if I gave anything less than my best effort, I wouldn't feel satisfied; I'd always know I'd had more to give. From the confusion and uncertainty around being entered in this event I hadn't expected, Wesley helped me get back on a level axis and then get energized for the race ahead.

We finally made our way to the starting blocks. "Runners, on your marks," the starter said, and Wesley helped me get situated. In my mind, I told myself, *When that gun goes off, be as explosive as possible. Get out of those blocks. This is it!*

The starter said, "Set."

Hips rose, feet against the blocks.

Bam! The gun went off, and we all started running. Because I was on the outermost lane, my starting point was farthest ahead. I couldn't hear anyone around me at the start of the race. As we approached the curve, athletes on the inner lanes pulled up closer beside me. I could hear everyone else to my left. As we rounded the curve and approached the straightaway, Wesley was talking the whole time: "Let's go!"

We got onto the straightaway. Our footsteps sounded like they were booming on the track. Maybe it was my heart beating. I could hear the other runners' spikes hitting the ground, so I had an idea of where they were.

Then it was like I blacked out those last few meters, using every last ounce of energy to throw myself across the finish line.

Wesley told me, "You got the bronze!"

It was so exciting and satisfying, being able to hop into that race and get a medal.

When we got back to the hotel room, I had time to sit there and think about our win. I knew deep down, Wesley deserved that bronze more than I did; I felt it in my heart. I gave that medal to Wesley. "I want you to have this," I said. "Without you, we wouldn't have gotten on that podium." It was Wesley who'd gotten us through the challenge, helping us rebound and have some success.

Wesley basically put his life on hold to work with me. But even though the guides train and run as fast as the athletes they're guiding, at that time guides weren't awarded medals of their own. The International Paralympic Committee changed this guideline in 2012 to award guide runners a medal as well. Even so, guides aren't awarded medals for their partnership in certain events. Wesley still does not receive a medal for assisting me in the long jump. This needs to change. Though guides aren't always tethered to an athlete, running their own sprints on the track, their role is integral to the success of the team.

Spectators may only see a guide standing at the end of the long jump, clapping and giving audible cues to the athlete, but the athlete has to be in a certain shape to be competitive. When I'm running sprints in training, Wesley is running those sprints with me. When I run hills, Wesley is charging up the hill alongside me. Just because he's "only" standing there at the competition doesn't mean he—or any other guide—hasn't put in hard labor leading up to that moment at the Games.

Capturing that medal in the 200 meters was a little bit of solace. In the end, we were able to achieve something we hadn't thought of—and Wesley was absolutely the reason I was able to do that. I was able to ride his wings to that finish line.

Lose Sight of Defeat

You have likely had a similar experience, some instance where you thought you were going to get something in your sphere of talent or genius, but it just didn't work out. Don't let those previous defeats create future losses.

Missing out on the opportunity to win my first long jump world title created a dark cloud for me. I was caught up in thinking, *We should have done this*, or *we shouldn't have done that*. Had I held onto those thoughts, it could have axed the success I had in the 200 meter.

Sometime after that, I went on to partner with a company called ViewSport, and together we released a line of shirts. One of the taglines on the front was "Lose Sight of Defeat." The shirt incorporated sweat-activated technology, so when the wearer perspired (and we would sweat a lot), a new message would appear on the back. Sweat hard enough in your "Lose Sight of Defeat" shirt and "Team LEX" would show up across your shoulders.

You have to get to a space where you can set aside the defeats and downfalls, challenges and negative things that happen in life. You have to lose sight of defeat so you can continue to find those new chances. Refuse to allow those previous challenges to impact what is in front of you, to impact potential opportunities and future wins.

Sometimes you have to shift your mindset from where you thought you were going, to where you actually are.

It was difficult to reframe that day because I felt like I did everything I could, yet whatever happened was beyond my control. It's much easier to be in a situation where I can put the blame on myself and assess what I did wrong. But to feel as though you've checked all the boxes and *still* fall short can be a difficult pill to swallow.

However, even when you have made a plan, everything can still go wrong, due to factors that were outside your control. That's when you need a *re-vision.*

There are many paths to the same goal, and sometimes you have to stop and take stock to understand what other options you might have. Just because one road dead-ends doesn't mean you can't get to your vision a different way.

Whatever path you choose, you will inevitably run into obstacles, challenges—even pain. You need the mindset to realize that dealing with those does not mean you've hit a dead end, it just means you need an alternate route to get to your vision.

So when things are looking bleak and dark, when the way you were going becomes too challenging, what can you do to cleanse your lens? Who can you connect with to get you back on the right path, or to help you have a different viewpoint of your route?

Training, No Matter What

When Wesley and I train together, we are right next to each other practically the entire time, almost like we're handcuffed together.

An average training session consists of us leaving our suite and walking to the track together, talking and having a good time. When we get down to our "Oval Office," we get our warm-up laps in and he's right beside me while we're running. Then we do drills, side by side: high knees, butt kicks, straight-leg shuffles, toe taps, and other dynamic exercises given to us by Coach Fischer.

Then we go to the long jump area, which is about the only time we're separated on the track. Wesley stands at the pit and claps and yells while I run, just like in competition. After the jumping portion, we do our running workout. That could be 150 meter repeats, hill runs, or any other brutal workout that Coach comes up with. Again, Wesley is running right next to me, doing everything I do.

In February 2020, we were ramping up our training, getting ready for the Games later that year. Excitement was running high.

And then March 2020 hit. This new virus we'd all been hearing about recently—COVID-19—created another hurdle.

In mid- to late March, we were told the Games would be postponed. They didn't tell us when, though, so we continued to train. At that point, we had to start to social distance, but we were still able to go down to the track.

Once the facility where I train detected the first positive COVID-19 test, however, we were locked down.

We had to quarantine in our rooms at the Chula Vista Elite Athlete Training Center (CVEATC). I shared a suite with a javelin thrower named Cody. We shared a common area, with a sofa, TV, refrigerator, and microwave, and we each had our own bedroom, bathroom, and closet. Because there were a number of positive COVID tests popping up on the complex, and because we didn't yet have a lot of information about the virus and how it spread, we both had to stay in our own rooms. It may sound spacious, but it felt small when we were stuck inside those walls all the time.

I suppose I could have gone home, but I didn't because I didn't want to put myself in jeopardy of catching the virus. I wasn't fearful of catching it myself—I was naive and figured that if I happened to catch it I'd be fine because I'm pretty healthy—but I didn't want to catch it at the CVEATC and bring it back to my mom, my grandma, and my family. I wasn't going to ride a train or bus all the way across the country; I would have flown, and being locked into a metal tube for four hours with recycled air seemed akin to licking a petri dish.

So I stayed in my room with the door shut, and every once in a while I heard Cody moving around—all of a sudden, he was the only person I had access to, and we weren't even supposed to be in the same room.

At mealtimes, we were sent the menu for the day, and we could text back whether we wanted option one, two, or three. Usually chicken, beef, and fish or pasta were in the lineup, with the same sides for each protein. Then our food was delivered to us. They would knock on the door to signal that the food was here. I was ready, listening for those knocks, every day between eight and nine for breakfast, eleven and noon for lunch, and five and six for dinner. Fortunately, we had a microwave, so we could reheat food if we didn't hear that knock. You really wanted to pick it up quickly if it was raining; otherwise, your food just sat there in its container, getting cold inside its soggy bag.

We were just cooped up for those first few weeks. I couldn't train, or even see anyone else. No visitors were allowed on campus, and Wesley was in his suite, while I was stuck in mine. There wasn't much we could do, other than watch YouTube and Netflix, or work on the computer. My sleep schedule was all thrown off. When quarantine first started, I would stay up until five or six in the morning, playing on the internet and falling down those YouTube rabbit holes, wide awake and checking out old movies. Then I'd sleep until breakfast came, eat, and then go back to sleep. I was just completely out of my regular routine.

There wasn't much information available yet about COVID-19, so we just stayed in our rooms until it was safe to come out. Everything had shut down. Events were postponed or canceled. I watched all the sponsorships and speaking engagements get wiped off the calendar. It was terrible. Track and field has given me so much, it's almost like the air in my lungs. The sport doesn't care about race, or abilities or disabilities; you're able to get out there and enjoy it regardless of the circumstances. To not be able to participate was one of the harder challenges I've been through.

At some point, my suitemate Cody ended up going home because he was a short-term resident, so then I was in the suite by myself from May until the latter part of the year.

Around the middle of May, I got approved to have an exercise bike in my room, so I could at least break a sweat *somehow*. (You just can't imagine how many laps it takes, running around a small living room, just to break a sweat!) My strength and conditioning coach helped me find a store online to purchase a medicine ball, resistance bands, and other equipment I could work with in the suite. We had to tap into the power of FaceTime so he could help me create a home workout regimen. I put my phone on a tripod and let him see the room, and he talked me through the setup for some of the exercises he wanted me to do.

We had to get creative with what I could do in the room. I knew I could do squat jumps, and I tested how much effort I could put into my takeoff—if I really exploded and popped up, would I hit my head on the ceiling? I never dented it, but I definitely grazed the top of my head a few times.

Eventually, they loosened the rules slightly and we were able to go outside and run on the Olympic path and the hills, but we still couldn't use the track or gym, and we were supposed to work out alone because they didn't want the athletes to congregate. When we were allowed out, I would go and run the stairs in addition to my in-room workouts. I got up early to exercise, and getting back out there to work out helped get my sleep schedule back in order.

I also had to take this same mindset and energy to the speaking side of things. My calling as a speaker had only started three or four years prior, and now it felt like my professional career was unraveling as I watched those engagements disappear and sponsor appearances get postponed and then canceled as the months of lockdown dragged on.

Making the move from in-person to virtual speaking was like another rebirth. I, along with so many other people, started to do everything on Zoom, Teams, and other virtual platforms. I turned the living room into my personal office, adding an adjustable desk so I could sit on my yoga ball or stand up like I was delivering a speech onstage. I learned all the new tactics and techniques for virtual presentations I could find. However, with everyone on mute,

I felt like I was talking to myself. It didn't matter if their cameras were on; I couldn't see them. I had no way of knowing whether they were engaged with what I was saying. I realized that I typically relied on verbal feedback to know if they were into the stories I told. Now, I didn't have that luxury.

What helped me through that time was remembering the lessons I shared in chapters 7 and 9, about using my voice as a guide and finding courage. Without the audience feedback—sniffles, laughter, crying—all I had was my own voice, so I began to be brave enough to become one with the narrative I would tell to the audience. I found myself telling these stories in a way where it almost didn't feel like I was talking about myself; I was just opening up and letting them come out of me.

Sharing my experience with a silent audience allowed me to be freer and go deeper. I let myself feel my emotions as I talked, and I found myself tearing up in certain parts. I never would have thought I'd have to deliver speeches from the computer—but in some ways, it ultimately created a more compelling experience with people who were listening and watching.

For months, I would do some training and then go into my living room office to deliver a speech. That got my wheels moving again, helped me gain momentum and desire to keep pushing forward.

Always Moving Forward

Sometimes when I was training on the campus, I would hear a voice yell, "Get it, Lex!" or, "Oh, yeah! Come on, bro. There you go!" It would be another athlete or staff member walking by and taking a moment to yell some encouragement. It was amazing to hear a familiar voice, that sound of someone in a similar situation—someone else who was sick of being stuck indoors and was doing what they could to grease the wheel for when competition could resume.

Eventually, we were told the Games wouldn't be canceled, they'd just be postponed until the following year, in August 2021. I wanted to stay in some sort of shape so I wouldn't have to start from zero.

I decided to find a place where I could run around at least a little bit on my own. I snuck out to the track early in the morning, when nobody else was around, so I'd have all the space to myself and wouldn't have to worry about social distancing. I used my cane to make my way down there, tapping into that same skillset I used when I was a kid mapping out the neighborhood. I found where the grass and the concrete meet the track.

That became my starting mark. I could feel the texture change under my feet. Then I paced out thirty meters, give or take. I slid my cane from side to side, making sure there weren't any obstacles in my way, nothing I could trip over or run into and hurt myself. Once I walked that space, I turned on a Bluetooth speaker and set it down at my end mark on the track. I played Pandora radio: Missy Elliot one day, Drake the next, Kendrick Lamar after that. With the music blaring, I knew where I was supposed to stop.

I didn't use a cane during workouts; all I had was the sound of the music and the feel of the grass line meeting the track. I had to be locked in, making sure I lined myself up on the border of the track, with the distant music directly ahead of me. These measures ensured I would run in a straight line and not deviate off course.

With those thirty meters paced out, I could do high knees, butt kicks, straight-leg shuffles. I could even get some accelerations in. Even though it wasn't training the same way I would have with Wesley, I was ensuring that when I got back on the track for real, I wouldn't have to start from scratch. That was my biggest goal.

I did that for a couple weeks, until one morning I heard a security guard call out, "Oh, man, I didn't know you were down here!"

He sounded startled and bewildered, like he wasn't sure if I should be there. We'd been given permission to walk around campus, jog the path, and run the stairs, but all the athletes had been instructed not to use any of the training venues. I heard the security guard leave, but then he came back a few minutes later and said, "You can't be out here, bro."

I'd already gotten my workout in, so I just said, "Alright, man. My bad, I'm sorry," and I left.

A couple days later, they gave us the green light to use outdoor training facilities. We could go down to the track again, but we still had to socially distance, training alone, not in groups. We still couldn't leave the campus unless it was for essential needs. My strength and conditioning coach was there to make sure the equipment was in the correct location for me. He coached from a distance, giving me audible cues on how to tweak my technique while doing weighted lunges, or medicine ball throws, or dumbbell squat jumps. He'd also give me verbal commands on how to navigate to the location of the next exercise.

Once we started to lift weights again, he would set up the barbells and add the correct weight to them. He gave me feedback on what I was doing well and what I needed to improve for each lift, all while following the rules and staying at a safe distance.

It wouldn't be until November or December—eight or nine months later—that Wesley and I were able to train together again. We'd trained together for thirteen years, and in that time we'd created a strong bond, which was suddenly broken during those months of separation. We didn't willingly disconnect—we were forced to do so—and it was tough, to say the least. We texted and talked on the phone, but it wasn't the same.

By the time we were able to train together again, we had already been told we weren't going to have the Games that year, so we could relax a little bit. But during a pandemic you can never completely let down your guard.

Are Your Barriers Real or Perceived?

Not being able to train with Wesley was a barrier for me—but was it a limitation to achieving my overall vision?

In that situation, I (along with everyone else) didn't have a lot of information about what was happening or what was to come. And that happens. We're not always going to have all the puzzle pieces. Sometimes we won't even have the instruction manual.

It's easy to think that we are limited by whatever is missing, that because we have encountered that first barrier, we won't be able to achieve our goals. But are we really limited, or is there a mindset shift that needs to happen?

We're bound to encounter setbacks in the pursuit of vision. But when we learn to think beyond our perceived limitations, we open up new possibilities to achieve our goals.

Even though I wasn't able to train with my guide, winning gold has always been a goal of mine. I feel, in a lot of ways, that it's bigger than me. It's my mom and Coach Whitmer, Wesley, and all the people who live through me.

Your goal may include all the people who follow your journey, who are rooting for you and want to see you do well.

We don't achieve anything in life without some assistance from other people. At times, I equate vision to people, because when we're born, so many people teach us and show us different perspectives. They enable us to see what's possible, to see our potential—and that helps to shape our outlook on life.

Once you lock into whatever your vision is, you will still need some assistance from others in order to achieve it. You will still have people who give you direction and help elevate you to new heights. As we grow and accomplish amazing things, those people deserve a piece of those accolades.

Giving in to perceived limitations, letting that vision go to waste, is to let those people down. You lose the opportunity to impact lives, instead of being able to push boundaries and find ways to rewrite the story while staying locked into what you see and believe.

When we have these causes that are greater than our individual selves, there has to be a way to push through the barriers, boundaries, and limitations—to figure out if those limitations even really exist in the first place.

Ask yourself, "Is this really a barrier? How can I continue to push the narrative, to move forward toward this huge vision of winning gold, even though the whole world is on pause?"

When a lot is occurring externally, we have to look for the eye in the middle of the hurricane. We can find a calm center, a safe haven, where we can access the strength and capability we need. I want you to be able to look at any situation and identify the space that you can carve out, where what you thought was a limitation or a barrier is moved aside so you are able to push forward, revising your plan and always moving toward your ultimate vision.

Have the confidence and courage to say to yourself, "This initial plan I had of the path leading toward my vision is not happening the way I needed it to. So now I need to switch up the plan, adapt and think creatively, carve out that thirty-meter space in the eye of the storm so I can maintain progress and momentum."

Use Previous Experiences as Your Guides

The COVID-19 pandemic impacted us all, directly and indirectly. Unfortunately, there have been a lot of lives lost because of the virus, and it put us all in a space where we had to live differently, changing our thoughts and actions.

I don't mean to equate the two, because they are not the same, but when I lost my sight I had a similar feeling: I suddenly wasn't able to access the world in the way I was used to, because everything had totally changed. So, during the pandemic, I had a sense of what it felt like when you can't access the world in ways you are used to. I had previous experience to look back to, to understand similar feelings I'd had in the past.

When I lost my sight, I was able to persevere because I got confidence from other people, who helped me learn to transition into this new space. March, April, and May of 2020, when I was cooped up in a room, unable to train or even hear my coaches' voices and teammates' laughter in person, were some of the worst months ever.

But because of my team of people who have been there for me, I have an ability to get through it even when the world is turned upside down.

You Already Know How to Bounce Back

We all have situations in our lives that we can look back on and say, "Even though this scenario is different, I have similar feelings now to those I had when I was in that space."

Are there any times you can point back to where you had similar emotions or challenges? Even though you're in a new, different situation, being able to rely on similar experiences can be helpful. How did you get through that situation? What was the outcome? Who were the people who helped you do that, and how exactly did they help you?

Reach for something similar so that even when times are challenging, you can refer back to the learning from your previous experience. Then apply some of those same actions and thought processes to get through the situation in front of you.

12

FOCUS ON THE WIN

In 2004, I went to my first Paralympic Games, in Athens, Greece, to compete in the long jump.

The long jump event took place on the first day of track competition, during the evening session. We got there early to warm up and prepare. I felt nervous anticipation, which is normal for me, but once I started moving around I was totally fine. My mindset was, *You're here right now, and this is an amazing opportunity—something that only a few people get to experience in their lifetimes.*

To be at the Games at such a young age, and after only participating in the long jump for two or three years, was major. I marveled at the accomplishment; I was so happy and proud to be there competing for the USA, representing my country while doing something that I love, I could hardly believe it was happening.

Then I snapped back into focus. I didn't have time for a rah-rah session; I had to compete! It was time to flip the switch, to get out there and perform.

My senses were heightened inside the stadium. I could feel my spikes gripping the surface of the track. I was aware that people were watching—a lot of people, more than I'd thought. I know that many people get nervous when they see a ton of people in one location, feeling like all eyes are on them. Fortunately, I didn't have to deal with that. Ever since I lost my sight, I've felt like everyone is *always* looking at me, wondering what I'm doing, where I'm going, if I need help. It was just another day of being scrutinized.

I could hear the crowd, of course, but I couldn't make out individual voices; the noise just all washed together in big waves of sound, of cheering, of people talking and yelling and being excited. I'm comfortable in front of large groups of people—it's only in smaller, more intimate settings that I start to get nervous—so I felt like I was in my element. I knew that a few of those voices belonged to my mom and grandmother, and Mr. Whitmer and his wife, who were all in the stands to watch me compete. That gave me a jolt of energy and ramped up my excitement to go out there and do something impressive.

In the long jump, we get six attempts to jump the farthest distance we can.

I already told you about my first jump, in Chapter 5, when I collided with Jerome.

I shook that off as best I could and jumped again. I knew I had to beat the marks the other jumpers had hit. When I landed, Jerome seemed excited, but I had only been working with him for about a month, so I didn't yet have a good understanding of his reactions. Then I heard my coach, Tony Veney, yell, "That's it!"

Coaches like Tony, who have been in the sport for a while, are able to gauge distances easily, and when an athlete has a significantly longer jump than the others, the coaches can see it.

The higher tone of Tony's voice told me that we'd landed a good jump.

After each athlete jumps, the official measures it and the mark is shown on a big screen. I knew what each person jumped immediately after they finished. When I'm behind the other marks, I know how far I have to jump in order to beat them. I look at those marks as my goal: I just need one good jump and I can leapfrog over everyone. Once you're the athlete with the best mark, however, everyone else is chasing *you*. If they hit that one good jump, they could potentially pass you up.

After I took my jump, there were still several other athletes left to jump after me. At that age, and because it was my first time at the Games, I was more focused on what everyone else was doing, checking out their results and marks. Back then, I thought, *I hope nobody passes me*, but over the years, as I've matured more, my thinking has shifted to, *I don't really care what everyone else jumps; I just need to make sure I execute my game plan. If someone just so happens to leapfrog me, then it'll be time for me to put myself in a position to respond. If I'm not in the number-one slot, that's cool. It only takes one jump.*

We all worked hard to get to this event, so it only made sense that we were going to be with people who put out some nice marks. Although it's rare, I've been in competitions where I've gone into the later rounds in the fifth- or sixth-place position, but one speedy run and monstrous jump catapulted me to the gold medal position. I love that, though I imagine it's deflating to everyone else in the field.

The age-old quote applies: "Life is 10 percent what happens to you and 90 percent how you respond." But at that first Games, I spent the time from when I jumped until the end of the event thinking, *Please don't pass me!*

My mark was 6.24 meters, and it held up to be the second-place mark. After the last athlete jumped and I realized I was going to be standing on that podium, winning silver,

I was pretty excited. Not only was it my first time going to the Games, but I had only been introduced to the sport a few years prior. I could still remember what it was like to try the long jump for the first time, how interesting and a little frightening it felt.

Then I thought back even further. Twelve years prior to those 2004 Paralympic Games, I had been in a hospital, unsure what the future held or how life was going to unfold without sight. I felt a deep sense of accomplishment and satisfaction that I had been able to overcome those specific fears around that disability, and make it all the way to representing my country.

During the medal ceremony, Jerome escorted me onto the podium. I stood there in anticipation, knowing that someone was going to walk up to me, shake my hand, and put the silver medal around my neck and the wreath on my head. I felt the young lady's presence as she approached. She placed the wreath gently on my head and handed me a bouquet of flowers. I stood there, receiving all of it, with Jerome by my side.

Just Getting Started

That first medal was only the beginning.

I didn't have a lot of expectations going into my first Paralympic competition: I just wanted to do my absolute best and see where the chips fell. Once I won silver, however, I saw what was possible.

After that first Paralympic Games, my dream to win gold became more clear. I was only one slot away, and I thought about my goal constantly. I saw a lot of the same competitors from the Games in other major international competitions, and I began to carve out a path for myself. That's when it started to come into focus: *I want to win the gold.* As I realized that could be a realistic goal, my thinking solidified: *I know I can win the gold.*

Winning means tapping into what you've got deep down inside you—and knowing you've exhausted yourself by giving everything you can. Once you've done that, there's nothing more you can do.

I'm a competitive person, I always want to win—for myself, of course, but also for other people. For as much time, effort, and energy as I've put into this career—and as much support, guidance, and advice I've received over the years—I have to be realistic and acknowledge that at some point, it will all have to end. The reality is that there's a lot more track and field behind me than there is ahead of me. So of course I really want to win a gold medal, not only for myself but for my supporters. For my mom and Mr. Whitmer. For the people who have devoted their time to helping me become the best athlete I can be. For Wesley, who devotes so much time to help me train. Wesley has never pressured me to feel like I have to win the gold; he always tells me to bring my absolute best, and the gold will come.

When you win, you get a feeling of satisfaction inside your soul—but that satisfaction is often only temporary. You're satisfied for the moment, but you know you still have more to achieve. I was satisfied when I won my first silver medal at the first Paralympics I participated in . . . but I wanted to experience that feeling again. I knew I wanted to go to the Games again, to get on the podium again—I wanted to *win* again. And next time I was on the podium, I wanted to win gold.

I'm fortunate. I've had the opportunity to participate in five Paralympic Games so far in my athletic career. I've won five silver medals, and each one has fueled my desire to push for gold. I've learned to celebrate each of those medals—some of which were harder to celebrate than others—while always pushing forward, to jump farther, win more, and make my dreams happen.

In 2008, I moved to San Diego, to the Olympic Training Center in Chula Vista, where I could wake up, train on a daily basis, and get access to incredible resources. I could get guidance from the best mental performance coaches, strength and conditioning coaches, and dieticians, all on campus. Everything was at my disposal, and I didn't require a car to take advantage of everything I needed in order to perform. I started to make it happen, to put myself in the best position to be able to win gold.

Beijing, 2008

A couple weeks prior to the Paralympic trials in 2008, I suffered a hamstring strain, so my performance at the trials was not to my liking. I saw the trainer every day that I was in Tempe, Arizona, for those trials. I received treatment for the injury daily, but the strain hampered my performance. I felt like I had this dark cloud looming over my head; I worried that I missed out on securing a spot on the team. The thought that I might not be able to go to the Games was too much to bear. Of course, it could have all been in my head—I don't know for certain if my spot on the team was ever actually in jeopardy, but it felt that way after my lackluster performance at trials.

Everything ended up working out, though. I made the team, healed up, and had my next opportunity to win gold.

The night before leaving for Beijing, I decided to pull an all-nighter so I could sleep on the plane. As I was finishing my preparation and packing, with about an hour and a half before the shuttle came at 4:00 a.m. to take us to the airport, I decided to lie down just for a minute. I told myself it would just be a quick catnap.

The next thing I knew, somebody was beating on my

door, yelling, "Hey, man, the bus is here! Everybody's down there. What are you doing?"

I grabbed my electronics and their chargers, my bags, and my rolling suitcase, and I ran for the bus. My teammate saved me from missing the bus. Whew!

We flew to Okinawa, Japan, to train for about ten days prior to the start of the Games. It's normal to fly out either to the host city or a city in close proximity to where the Games are being held, so the athletes can get acclimated to the country and being in a new time zone.

This was my second time going to the Games; I had one under my belt, and I felt like it was going to be a great competition. Not only was I competing in the long jump, I was also competing in the triple jump and running the 100, 200, and a leg of the 4x100meter relay.

The long jump competition was fantastic—and fierce. I was chasing one of the athletes from China: my mark was right behind his, and I had one jump remaining to try and pass him up.

I got on the track, on the start mark. At that point, I was taking sixteen strides to cover the distance from the start mark until I jumped.

I started running, and for whatever reason—I don't know if I just lost track of the number of strides—I jumped too soon. I took off on my fourteenth stride, still a few feet away from the take-off zone. As soon as I left the ground,

I immediately knew that I'd made a mistake. Fortunately, I still landed inside the sand pit. They measured my mark, from what I remember, at 4.6 or 4.8 meters. I lost all that distance because I didn't jump from the correct spot—if I had, I very well could have won the gold I was searching for; it felt like an extremely long jump.

The athlete from China was able to hold on, and with the mark from one of my previous attempts, I earned silver.

That was one of the few competitions where I was kicking myself, where I felt like I left something on the table. But I knew that I was the one who messed up, no one else. I was able to swallow that pill because I had to take full responsibility for my mistake. I secured the silver, and I had total closure; it was no one's fault but my own.

The jump may have felt explosive and powerful, but at the end of the day, I still needed to execute correctly. I just had to make sure I didn't allow that to happen again.

I would tap into everything I could control to learn from that mistake and never repeat it.

London, 2012

I went into the London Paralympic Games feeling like, "Third time's a charm!" It was another opportunity to keep pushing and moving toward that gold.

Between 2008 and 2012, I had come out with my slogan,

"No need for sight when you have a vision," and within that time I had introduced this line to the world. I started putting more focus into speaking, branding, and marketing, and I had some great energy going on. In 2011, I broke the world record in the long jump. I had my fastest 100 meter time going into 2012. I felt like I was unstoppable!

The next piece of the puzzle was going to London and doing what I needed to do in competition.

In June of 2012, we were invited to Vancouver, Canada, to participate in a circuit (a number of meets all in one location). While there, I ran the 100 meters.

In one of our competitions, I waited in the blocks, ready to race. The announcer called, "On your marks, set, go." *Pow*, the gun went off. We were out of there. I was running, driving hard down the track. Just as I was about to transition into the upright position, I felt a pop in my quad and I fell to the ground.

That dreaded pop is the one sound every athlete fears. I was so scared. Sure, I'd strained my hamstring back in 2008 and I'd had a few injuries that kept me off the track for a few days, but nothing very serious. Now I felt something wrong with my leg—I'd fallen down—but I didn't really know what was going on. The Paralympic trials were the very next week. *Was I going to be able to compete? How would this impact me going forward? Was winning the gold now out of reach?*

I wasn't able to finish the race. We went to the middle of the field where the trainers did a quick examination and said it could be a couple scary options, possibly even a torn Sartorius muscle. I was booked on the next flight home.

The next day, Wesley helped me through the airport and we flew back to San Diego, to the Olympic Training Center. The sports medicine building was closed, but given my injury, they opened it up so the doctors there could do a more thorough exam. The staff was waiting for us when we arrived. After an MRI, they told me I had a grade two/three quad strain, which meant there was separation in the muscle. They assured me it would take a few weeks to heal, but I'd be totally fine.

I was off the track for a month, during the time period of trials and preparing for London. Fortunately, we have a discretionary process where a small number of people can be considered for the team without going through trials, given extenuating circumstances. Knowing that it was an injury I could come back from with enough time to prepare for London, having an athletics resume that showed all the major international competitions I'd competed in, and being a medal winner all helped. I acquired one of the discretionary spots.

I hadn't been off the track for that long, ever. Not being able to train, to participate in the event I love, was brutal—and not being able to compete because my body physically wouldn't allow me to was even worse.

I was used to my body operating a certain way. Once I was injured, I started questioning myself and my abilities. Would I still be able to lift weights and run fast? Could I still do all the things I was accustomed to? It seemed like my future was so uncertain.

By mid-July, I was able to slowly get back on the track again. I wasn't able to keep up my regular training, especially endurance and speed training, so I lost some of my lung capacity. There were plenty of times in the lead-up to London when we were working out and I felt like I was dying, but everybody else was fine. The coaches and other athletes would stand on either side of the track and cheer me on: "Come on, Lex!" It was awesome to have that encouragement.

It got to the point where my physical therapist and all the professionals who were helping me recover said everything was good and I'd healed up fine. They loosened the leash a little more, told me I could go out and push harder. Mentally, I was still questioning: *Would I still be able to compete at a high level?*

That mentality followed me into the Games, making my participation even more challenging.

Getting injured as I was trying to prepare for one of the biggest competitions of my life is one of the major setbacks I've encountered while trying to pursue my vision.

I had to lean on those people who fueled my vision. I reached out to people who had dealt with injuries before, asking, "How did you deal with it? How did you think and feel and push forward? Did you also feel fear and uncertainty around not being able to perform to the best of your ability?"

When you encounter similar setbacks, leverage your network, your team, so you can work through that challenge. They can help get you to a space where you have some relief; you can exhale knowing that you have a challenge, but it can be overcome. Listen to them, and follow their lead. As with anything else, it takes some work, energy, and tenacity to get through setbacks. Be patient and understand there's a process that needs to be followed. Otherwise, if you let it, the mental aspect will make you feel like you're just going in circles.

When we got to the competition, I knew I'd had a setback, but I told myself to go in there and make it happen. I did my best, given the circumstances, but unfortunately, I didn't win the gold.

But I left the competition healthy, and I did everything I could do physically and mentally on that day—and I still made it to the podium, taking home another silver. I'll always look back on that competition with a smile on my face. My injury had taken me off the track for a month, and within the remaining month and a half before the Games, I was able to bounce back and leap onto the podium. I count that as a win.

Rio, 2016

In 2013, I won three medals in Lyon, France—including my first world championship and gold medal at a major international competition, in the long jump; silver in the triple jump; and silver as a member of the 4x100-meter relay team.

After my final jump, I was leading the competition with only one other athlete who had one jump remaining. I waited off to the side with my heart in my throat, thinking, *Man, don't you dare snatch this away from me!*

He jumped...and he didn't pass my mark. As soon as the other jumper landed in the sandpit, my coach yelled from the stands, "Congratulations, champ!" I was so happy to hear him yell that. Wesley came up and slapped me on the back. It was official: I was a gold medal winner! That was a breakthrough for me—up to that point, it had been silver medal city. To be able to get on top of that podium felt like I got the monkey off my back—but now I needed gold at the Paralympics.

In 2015, I went on to win gold at the Parapan American Games, which was one of the best competitions of my life. Because it's a regional competition, involving nations from

North, Central, and South America, there aren't always enough athletes within a disability category to fill the event. When that happens, they combine a couple categories together, so our category of blind and visually impaired athletes was grouped together with the next category up—which meant we were competing against athletes who had sight. That win meant a lot to me because I out-jumped *everybody*, sighted or not. I tied the world record and set a new Parapan American Games record. It made me even more satisfied to know that there were athletes out there who could see but they still could not beat me that day. It was a great competition.

I also won gold at the 2015 World Championships. I point out all these competitions because I was telling myself, *Alright, since Lyon, France, I haven't finished less than gold. We have Rio coming up. Although I'm not going to underestimate my competitors, if I execute then I should be able to continue the streak and win that elusive gold medal I want so badly.*

In the previous four years, from 2012 to 2016, I got more into speaking, became a brand ambassador for a number of companies, and even shot some TV commercials. It was setting up to be the perfect ending to the four-year quad.

That year, the Paralympic trials took place in Charlotte, North Carolina—in my home state. A lot of my family and friends hadn't yet seen me compete in person, so they drove down from Raleigh and surrounding areas to watch me. I was on cloud nine.

From there, over the next couple months training for the Games in Rio, I told myself, "This is it, right here. This is the fourth time. All the times before meant that you're not far off. You have the ability and the capacity to win this. Let's go out there and make it happen!"

The night before a major competition, I watch one of two movies: *Remember the Titans* or *Dark Knight*. The night before competing in Rio, I watched *Dark Knight* to help me get into the zone. I envisioned myself as the superhero with a calculating opposition force to be defeated.

I was scheduled to compete on the first day of track and field competition, in the morning session. We made our way to the stadium. By now, I was accustomed to the process: going through a warm-up on the track, getting loose. Eventually they announced our event over the loudspeaker and we went to the call tent. I heard the familiar voices of the athletes I'd been competing against for years. I just knew this was going to be the day.

Once we got into the stadium, we had a period of time to do our warm-up runs on the long jump runway. The announcer was talking over the PA system and they played loud music, so I couldn't hear anything but noise. I asked Wesley to talk to the officials who would be running the long jump, to see if they could turn it down, but they said there was nothing they could do about it. It was difficult—I already can't see, so if I can't hear anything, I'm left totally disoriented and lost. Not being able to hear my guide amplified those feelings. I told myself, *You've been doing this for a while, just go ahead and get a safe mark in, at least make sure you make it to the next round to have a shot at the gold. Don't stress, it'll be fine.*

Those first couple jumps were not good at all. I believe I was in tenth place, which was unfamiliar territory for me. When I got to the third jump, I knew I had to get a decent mark—in the top eight, at least—so I could go on to the final round. I couldn't just try for a safe mark anymore; I had to go for it.

I was standing on the track. I didn't feel nervous. I told myself I'd give it my all, to make this happen. I ran and jumped, and my mark was good enough to skyrocket me from tenth place up to sixth.

I had three jumps remaining. It was time to let it all out.

The fourth jump was okay. In my fifth jump, I went from sixth place to first, with a distance of 6.44 meters. I wasn't ready to claim a victory yet; I still had one jump left, and I knew I needed to exceed my previous mark by a good amount to put the competition in the bag.

Going into that sixth and final round, I was still in the lead. As I'd been waiting on the sidelines for my turn to come back around, Wesley walked over to tell me the noise was wreaking havoc on other athletes, too. Each of us had sixty seconds to complete an attempt, and the noise from the crowd made it difficult to hear. Many of the athletes chose to stand and wait until it was quiet, and some athletes ran out of time trying to coordinate with their guides. The sixty-second clock expired, and the attempt was counted as a foul or no mark.

I went out there for that final jump, thinking, *You gotta make this one count*. In my mind, 6.44 meters was not a safe mark.

When I took my first couple steps, the crowd broke out into even louder chaos and commotion. Not being able to hear Wesley made the long jump as difficult to navigate as a sprint would be if someone had cut our tether. I wanted to stop, but I was in the middle of my run and I had picked up so much speed and forward momentum that I didn't think I could hit the brakes before getting to the take-off zone—and if you touch the take-off zone, you have to jump or it's considered a scratch.

I was almost to the board, so I continued running and jumped like normal. When I landed in the sand, I didn't have a good feeling about that mark. It made me uneasy because I knew I hadn't put the competition out of reach; if anyone else leapfrogged me, they would win the gold.

And that's exactly what the very last jumper did. When the Brazilian athlete came out for his jump, the announcer came on the loudspeaker and hushed the crowd. The stadium went quiet. I could hear the guide's voice boom out over his crisp claps to cue the long jumper. As any poised athlete would do, he executed well. After the Brazilian's jump, the crowd's cheers confirmed it: he won the gold.

That one hurt. In my silver win in Beijing, I was fine putting the blame on myself. And if it had been my fault—if I had skipped out on a bunch of training sessions or been slacking off in the weight room—I would have accepted that, too. But in this competition, I felt like external factors were a large part of why the other competitors and I weren't able to compete to the best of our abilities. We were at the pinnacle of competition for athletes: we want people to see the best event ever, not athletes who were hindered by external factors. It was difficult for me to do my absolute best.

I replay that competition a lot in my imagination. If we'd been able to have silence during the event, it could have been different. That's not a foreign concept; it's often afforded to us, because that's an essential part of being able to compete.

I learned a lesson from that experience: if that type of situation ever occurred again, I would be more adamant in my request to have something changed. Maybe I should have stood in the middle of the runway, refused to let the competition go on—not just for me, but for everybody. I didn't want to beat someone who was hampered by a circumstance like crowd noise; I wouldn't be able to fully cherish a win in that circumstance. Hearing is an essential factor for success for we athletes who are blind. I wanted all of us out there, doing our best, under the best possible conditions, so whoever won knew they beat me fair and square—not because I couldn't hear my guide.

At the time, my perception was that this was outside my control, that there was nothing I could change. Now, I think I could have done something different. I could have waited to start until they got the message that the crowd needed to be quieter. Whether those things would have been successful, and whether they would have made the difference, is another story—but at least I could have tried.

This One's for You

Since becoming a speaker, I've received hundreds of emails, letters, and thank-you notes from people telling me how what I've taught them has helped them.

When I was just talking about myself, telling my story, the feedback was much different.

It's not terrible to hear, "you're amazing," "you're so inspiring," or "you're so brave," but after adjusting my presentations to make them more about the people listening, their responses became more about times *they* took a risk, how *they* learned to look at situations differently, or how *they* were able to get that extra nudge they needed to keep going. The feedback shifted from being about me to being about *them* and what they were going to do as a result.

At no time did I feel this more than when, during a virtual Q&A session after a speech, a parent asked me, "What advice would you give my seven-year-old kid who has endured five heart operations?"

First of all, I would say that seven-year-old is a warrior, an absolute champion. And then I told them that I could relate. I had ten operations on my eyes when I was eight years old. It was so difficult and scary, and that was just on my *eyes*, not a heart that you need to live.

I'd go into the hospital and they'd tell me that everything was going to be fine. And then another doctor would tell me that I needed yet another operation—but it was going to be alright. That's what they told me the first time! And the second, and third, and fourth. What would make this time any different?

I was scared of not being able to see again, but I was also frightened that I'd only be able to see how I could at the time. Everything was disfigured, and with each operation, my sight changed—sometimes shifting my gaze upward made everything darker; other times, gazing downward looked like I was seeing everything through bubbles.

I was afraid of being stuck with that eyesight, and I wondered, *Is it worth it to see things like this...or would it be better to just not see anything at all?*

That fear was debilitating. It was paralyzing. I didn't want to do anything: I just wanted to stay in one spot, away from other people who might ask questions about my eyes. People who had never seen someone who looked different stared at me, and although I didn't think they meant for it to be negative, all those eyes locked on me made me feel uncomfortable.

Even later, when I couldn't see them, I knew people were staring at me when I walked into a room. They may have been wondering, *What do we do? How do we help him?* People asked, "What can you see? How much can you see?"

As an eight-year-old—and certainly by the time I went back to school at nine or ten years old—these questions were embarrassing and felt shameful. I felt small. Going to school, I would walk into a classroom and stop as I assessed where to go, and I could hear the normal chatter die down as everyone looked at me. Those are difficult feelings for a young kid to have. You want to be part of the group, to feel cool, not to be the kid who is friendless and isolated, who eats lunch alone, just listening to the other kids laughing and having a good time.

That seven-year-old kid was dealing with far more difficult operations than I had... but I also had to imagine some of our experiences were very similar, as two young kids facing overwhelming adversity in life. It is so scary to have to go inside that hospital and not fully understand what's happening or whether you're going to be okay. He probably missed a lot of school, spending that time with his parents instead of his friends.

Even when he was able to go back to school, he might not have built solid relationships with his peers, so he's the new kid. If he had to use any kind of assistive equipment, that further set him apart as different. Younger kids don't really understand, and they stare. He likely looked around at all those eyes looking back at him and wondered, "What are they thinking about me?"

Then the moderator said, "When you win the gold in Tokyo, you'll have to shout him out!"

"Of course," I told them. "When I win the gold, I'm going to dedicate it to my new friend because he's awesome. He is the shining example of what it means to go through some really tough times, so my gold medal jump is dedicated to him because he deserves it."

I wanted to give him the motivation that comes with knowing he has another person who believes in him. I wanted him to have that feeling, that a world-class athlete he looks up to took the time to give him some advice and dedicate a special moment in time just for him. That might be the very inspiration he needed to keep moving forward, to take whatever action he envisions for his life.

The least I can do as a person and an athlete is share

a moment with someone else. Being able to dedicate that competition to him would be something for him to hold onto, something a doctor couldn't prescribe.

Tokyo, 2020

I thought about that kid over the next few weeks in preparation for Tokyo. I played out in my head how I was going to shout out, "My man!" I got excited imagining him watching and smiling, feeling special that he was getting that shout-out and knowing that I kept my word.

We arrived safely in Tokyo, and training sessions went very well. The morning of the competition, I checked out *Remember the Titans*. I'm always inspired by how Denzel Washington's character, Coach Boone, finds a way to overcome his obstacles, no matter how many darts or rocks are thrown at him. I love the way he gets the team to work together given their differences in race, background, and culture.

It was almost time to compete. I put on my uniform, got on the bus, and headed to the stadium. I was pumped up.

When I got to the stadium, it felt like being at a high school track meet again. There weren't any fans in the stands. There weren't many people there at all. I know it was for COVID safety, and I was glad we were even having the Games, given the pandemic. I could still feel the magnitude of the competition, I just couldn't hear many people around me.

Wesley and I warmed up, which didn't take long because it was so hot and humid. We chatted a bit with my coach in preparation for battle.

Eventually we were instructed to go to the call room. When we put on blindfolds, they make us put gauze over our eyes first. This became a rule around 2017 or 2018. The gauze serves as a second layer to ensure all athletes are in fact totally blind. But I forgot to grab the gauze before we went to the call room, so Wesley had to run and grab some from our team tent, which was no short trek. When Wesley returned, I could tell he'd booked it, because he was short of breath. The officials checked our gauze and blindfolds, then escorted us to the warmup track, where they checked our shoes. Finally, we were led into the stadium to prepare for competition.

I had some great practice runs on the track. The surface under my spikes was extremely fast. There was no crowd, so I knew we'd be okay from a sound standpoint; I wouldn't have the same situation as five years ago. I felt good.

On my first jump of the competition, I fouled—just barely, stepping no more than an inch over the front of the take-off board, but a foul nonetheless. I landed in the sand, stood up, and walked toward the back of the pit, hoping it wasn't actually a foul, but Wesley told me it was. If it hadn't been, I feel my mark would have been great, because when I stood up to walk toward the back of the pit, it only took a step or so. I was still hyped. *Today might be the day you jump the entire length of the pit!* I thought. This was going to be a good day.

The track was fast. Whatever surface they use at the Games, combined with adrenaline, energy, and mojo you have going on, means that you're moving differently, faster, which can put you in a position where you might barely take off past the board. My coach gave me great feedback on how I was looking in the competition, and we moved my start mark back a little bit to allow for the speed I was bringing down the track. The extra room would help eliminate any more fouled attempts.

We had a few intermissions for medal ceremonies and other events, which created a lot of noise, so they'd pause the long jump until those were completed. Nick, one of my teammates and suitemates at the Athlete's Village in Tokyo, had raced earlier and won the gold; he was now having his medal ceremony. When they played the national anthem for him, I thought to myself, *That's about to be me in a couple hours!* That was some extra motivation during the event itself. Wesley and I were getting excited.

Finally, it was my sixth jump. Last one, best one. I was unclear what position I held in the rankings, but I knew I wasn't in first. I stood on the track, making sure I followed the same pattern that had typically resulted in big jumps: being patient in the beginning when I start to run, making sure that I'm driving out and very powerful with those first strides, then slowly starting to transition to an upright position, running tall, and then getting ready to jump.

I felt like my run was good. I jumped. But when I landed in the sand, I knew it wasn't good enough to win gold. I wasn't paying attention to the other marks; I was basing my success on how I knew I jumped.

When I woke up the next morning, after winning silver in Tokyo, I saw all these text messages, emails, and social media mentions from people congratulating me, but I just felt sad. I had set my mind on achieving something, and it didn't happen. That's tough anytime, but what made it even tougher was that I had five chances to achieve that goal. These opportunities don't come every day, only once every four years, and I'd had seventeen years. That hurt. I wanted to win, for that little boy, for Wesley, and yes, for myself.

Because of COVID, the medal ceremony had to operate in a different fashion. Usually, in competitions in the past, an official is on the stand to put the medals around our necks. That year, they handed the medals to the guides and had the guides put the medals around the athletes' necks. That stung extra—not that Wesley was giving me the medal, but because I wanted Wesley to be putting a gold medal around my neck.

After the Games were over, I wanted those headlines to be different. I wanted to achieve my goal. When I saw all those "congratulations on silver" messages, it was like the word silver was emphasized, amplified. I didn't hear anything else; all I heard was *silver, silver, silver*. I just wasn't in a space at that time where I was happy about how everything turned out.

It Still Isn't Over

When something means a lot to you, you continue to go after that goal until you achieve it. Make no mistake about it: I'm locked into winning gold, and I'll do everything in my power to win it in Paris in 2024. There's only one more step to go. That's not that much, especially when I consider that I could have not gotten on the podium, or even made it on the team at all.

A large part of winning is never giving up. Mentally, tell yourself to get up, keep pushing forward. Tell yourself, *I gotta keep going, keep fighting, keep working*. When you choose not to quit, you're already experiencing some level of what it means to win.

Dig deep and focus on the winning elements. Sometimes winning feels binary—you either get the gold or you don't. But in actuality, you can always find the areas of your life where you did have a win. Focus on those moments, let them give you the inspiration and motivation to keep going. All isn't lost. You're on the doorstep to realizing your vision.

Find the things you did correctly: these winning elements become the wind beneath your wings to achieve in the future.

CONCLUSION

During the COVID-19 pandemic, when everything went virtual, I began doing my blindfold workshops a different way.

First, I have my participants put on blindfolds. Then I immerse them in the experience of a day in Paralympic competition.

Imagine yourself in Tokyo. You're standing on the long jump runway, the red track stretching out in front of you. Eighty thousand pairs of eyes are watching you. There is a hush over the stadium; it's completely silent. Feel the rubberized surface under your feet. You have your spikes on, and you can feel them gripping the ground. You hear your guide yell out, "Are you ready?" Focus and lock into the sound of your guide's voice. The guide begins to clap and yell as loud as he can.

At the right moment, you push off with both legs and begin moving down the track toward your guide's voice and clapping hands. *One stride, two strides, three, four.* You gradually pick up speed, feeling the slight breeze on your face. *Five, six, seven, eight.* Now you approach a full-on sprint, fast as your body can possibly go. You pump your arms vigorously and lift your knees to a ninety-degree angle. *Nine, ten, eleven, twelve.* You blaze down the track. Your guide's voice and clapping hands sound like they're right in front of you now, so close it almost seems you'll run into them. *Thirteen, fourteen, fifteen.* It's almost time. This is your last step. *Sixteen... time to fly.*

At this point, as you soar through the air, ask yourself: where do you want to land?

I want you to walk in these shoes and experience each moment as I would, using your senses to understand your environment, feeling the track's surface under your feet, listening to your guide's yelling voice and the crowd's roar of admiration as you land in the sand.

Envision yourself back at the take-off point. Identify what it is that prohibits you from taking your leap. What risks are you afraid of? We all find ourselves at points in our lives when we need to take a risk, but so often we wear blindfolds that prohibit us from seeing things with more clarity.

Take off your blindfold. Now write down the one thing that is serving as a blindfold in your life. Identify your limitations or boundaries. For example, "When hard times arise, I can reach down deep to find my resilience." Or, "I tend to dim my light too much, so everybody else can shine, and sometimes I want to get a little credit, too."

When you remove that blindfold, it is like you're taking off whatever is limiting you.

Remove Your Blindfold

This blindfold exercise is about identifying the roadblocks that can exist in our paths. I've found that in most cases, this activity is about accessing more empathy, equity, and understanding of what we can do to help meet others where they are so they're in the best position to succeed. What obstacles, challenges, mindsets, and perceptions interfere with our ability to see ahead with clarity and truth? Where are the areas we're wearing blindfolds?

Our blindfolds keep us from seeing our true potential, or the progress we're making toward achieving our vision. There are also blindfolds in our culture, especially when it comes to conscious and unconscious biases around race and ability. Engaging in discussions on these issues helps us remove our blindfolds and find ways to break down systems and structures that have marginalized different groups across the country.

How can we remove our own blindfolds, so we view a given scenario as it should be viewed, instead of the way it appears through our limited perceptions? How can we encourage others to remove their blindfolds as well? The answer is through developing our vision. When we can set our sights on the amazing, incredible goal we're aiming for in the distance, we can begin to see the obstacles, perceptions, and biases that tend to hold us back from it. Removing the blindfold allows us to create stronger, inclusive, equitable relationships that help us join together and burst through to a brighter future.

Leaders who participate in this exercise have a greater understanding of how to move forward with sensitivity. They have specific items they need to improve. To achieve the same results, you have to be open and honest about what your roadblock is, and what is specifically inhibiting you and your team. You have to identify it and write those words down on the blindfold. Commit yourself and your team to working on these obstacles daily, to turn your words into action.

If you're in a situation where some materials are not as accessible for someone on your team, you can take a few minutes to help them so it doesn't continue to be an issue for them. Give them the tools necessary to do their job—and ultimately help the team progress forward.

Great leaders understand that limitations exist separately from the person, and they can look deeper and figure out a way to adjust, adapt, and tear things down to build them back up. You may have a fantastic team equipped with the skills you need to push your business forward—but *they* have to also be equipped with the best resources to continue that progress.

Really great leaders will look to themselves before pointing the finger at anyone else. Just like the Michael Jackson lyrics, "working on the man in the mirror," they ask where there may be flaws, inconsistencies, or things to be improved.

A leader may assume they know what needs to be done and what a team member needs in order to help them do it, but a great leader reaches out and asks what another person's experiences are, so they can tailor what they do based on what they hear from the person. We can't make assumptions. When you ask questions from a place of curiosity and interest in learning, you throw the ball into the person's court and let them make a decision about what they need to share with you, so you can step into that space and assist the best way possible without making that person feel uncomfortable.

You're looking at the world through your own experiences and what you've had to deal with in the past. But when you are able to get vulnerable and open up about the challenge, obstacle, or figurative roadblock that impedes your progress and performance, you remove that blindfold—and then you are able to step around anything in the way of achieving your vision.

A Journey to Vision

Throughout this book, you've seen examples from my story of breaking through perceived limitations. You've learned that there is no need for sight when you have a vision. Let's take a look back at that journey.

Map what you know to explore the unknown: As I lost my sight, I was able to continue to see the same neighborhood I was previously able to see and navigate—but now I see it in a different way. You might lose something, but you can see that scenario from a different angle, which can help you to continue pushing forward toward your vision. On the other side of blindness was vision. On the other side of roadblocks is open opportunity.

Become numb to no: I don't want you to hear "no" and have that serve as a stop sign. No can just mean "not yet" or "not me," that it's just not the right time or person to help you with this particular issue. But you can find another solution, without stopping. There is a *yes* out there, and you have to keep pushing forward and keep working, doing everything in your power to discover that yes.

Stop worrying about blending in—or standing out: Don't be distracted by being different or the same. As you pursue your vision, you might see similarities and ways you are different, but that's a natural progression of moving forward organically toward your vision. Stay aligned with your vision and your authentic self, rather than getting distracted trying to fit in or stand out.

Are you a catalyst?: Are you an agent for change? If not, should you be? Think about what Mr. Whitmer did: Do you have the courage to step out there, to blaze a trail and provide that light in the darkness, to be the voice of sanity in a space where there is an overwhelming amount of doubt and questioning? Are you able to stay locked in and know confidently where you want to go and where you want to take others? When you're a catalyst, a lot of people may not see your vision, and they may ridicule you or question you. But true catalysts don't care about that because they are so driven by what they see ahead. As that gap between them and their vision decreases, the rest of the world is able to see what the catalyst has seen all along. I want you to have the courage to keep pushing forward, and when you're adamant about it and you truly believe it, it will become a reality, and what was once blind to others will be revealed.

Set your vision: I want you to see beyond your horizon, and be able to help another see that vision, help them to paint their life's portrait. That's the beauty of vision: it looks different to each person you share it with—but ultimately it's about being able to see beyond what's in front of your eyes. That takes a lot of trust in yourself. When you look at the gap between where you are now and where your vision is, it may look so distant and far off. Set the vision and have the trust to put one foot in front of the other to close that gap . . . at which point you can wrap your arms around what you saw all along! Mr. Whitmer saw that I had an idea of what was possible, and he continued to strike that match until the fire consumed my mind's view. When we have things to look forward to, it keeps that fire lit, keeps us wanting more. Once you set that vision, you will do whatever it takes to see it transform to reality.

Vulnerability is the key to effective teamwork: Open communication is key to deepening your partnerships and developing shared trust. As you collaborate with others, it's important for you to be vulnerable and direct about what you need, so you can bring in people who can help you get to your goal.

Who fuels your vision?: When we talk about setting your vision and the trust it takes to move toward it, I want you to understand you don't have to do it alone, and quite frankly, you *can't* do it alone. A true authentic vision is meant to transform minds, it's meant to transform culture in the world. You might be the match that starts that fire, but in order for it to grow and become a furious blaze, you need to work with other people. That means adding more layers to your trust, to trust others and their abilities so you can continue to close that gap between where you are and where your vision is.

Your voice is a guide: I want you to understand that words are powerful. Stories are powerful. Experiences are powerful. If you have the vulnerability at times to share those pains or struggles, you can positively impact the lives of other people. And you don't have to be onstage to do that. A lot of times we are able to make forward progress just knowing that someone else has been through a similar situation. Hearing their vantage point helps expand our own thinking. You can be that voice for someone, the person who shares those experiences in a way that serves as a lesson, helps them avoid mistakes and roadblocks, and guides them through understanding their place in their own unique challenges in life.

Move mountains by learning to feel: I don't want you to just be locked into things that are fixed, like numbers or routines. At some point, something within you has to just say, "This feels *good*!" Focus on the feeling, even if you don't know logically why it feeds your vision. It didn't make "sense" to throw a baseball at the wall as a kid—I wasn't going to be a professional baseball player—but it felt good. It was fun. It made me *feel* something. In the end, the skills I built culminated in my athletic career. I swapped out the World Series for the World Championships.

Your courage is just beyond your fear: I discovered that beyond blindness was a world full of infinite possibilities. For you, blindness might be a synonym for fear. When you're at the doorstep of fear, though it may feel uncomfortable, that is a really great place to be, because growth and development is right in front of you. Being able to walk through that doorway of fear leads you to a space where you can grow, expand, and develop. Tapping into that courage is what allows you to be able to push forward even in the face of challenges.

When vision needs a revision: Somewhere along this road of achieving your vision, you might find yourself in a position where there needs to be a change or adaptation. Understand that needing to revise, to get back on that path toward what you want to achieve, toward your vision, is okay. It might appear as though things are completely different and you might feel like you've been thrown into the spin cycle. But building off that courage you have from crawling over that fear will help you see you need to make a change—and that's going to get you locked back onto the path you had been following.

Focus on the win: I operate in a space where wins are determined by seconds on the track and meters or centimeters in the sand, and my job is always to outdo my competitors when the time calls for it. However, real winning comes when you get that internal, gut-satisfying feeling of "I achieved this." No matter what it is you want to achieve in life, we all know that feeling of massive satisfaction and completion.

So, what have we learned?

Never allow sight to overpower your vision. Sight and vision are always at war with each other; you see something now and think, "I see that, I want that." You might sacrifice what you see in front of you for what is on the horizon before it exists. But sight is constantly changing. When you wake up, it could be gloomy outside, or it might be sunny.

Vision, on the other hand, doesn't change; you have a unique vision for success or for the world. No matter how amazing or difficult things may look, that vision is what carries you through any of those moments, and gives you inspiration, hope, and motivation even during times of turmoil. That's the epitome of the title of this book.

This may sound strange, but I am grateful for blindness. Because I couldn't rely on my sight, I learned to develop vision, and that process has revealed so many benefits in my life that I never would have imagined. When I first lost my sight, my blindness felt like my enemy, but it has turned out to be one of my most gracious and giving friends.

At times, the world is a dark place for all of us, but I want you to tap into your ability to imagine an incredible goal for yourself. Conjure up the energy you need to turn it into reality. You'll need courage, adaptability, and a relentless mindset to bring your vision to fruition. When you're able to truly see your dream in front of you, you'll see the whole world differently.

ABOUT THE AUTHOR

LEX GILLETTE is the most recognized and accomplished totally blind long and triple jumper in the history of the US Paralympic movement. The world record–holder in long jump and a five-time Paralympic medalist, he's a co-founder of Sight School, a nonprofit teaching the visually impaired to see their potential through educational resources, employment initiatives, and athletic opportunities. Lex also serves on the board of directors for the nonprofit Classroom Champions, an organization that leverages the mentorship of world-class athletes to improve student engagement, build growth mindsets, and inspire positive classroom culture.

CPSIA information can be obtained
at www.ICGtesting.com
Printed in the USA
JSHW021943160423
40418JS00001B/1